THE AESTHETIC SHIFT

The Aesthetic Shift

VINCENT BOZZINO

The Aesthetic Shift. Value Corruption and Normative Conflict.
© 2025 by Vincenzo "Vincent" Bozzino

Libertine Press
34 Berkeley Square
London, UK W1J5BF

www.libertinepress.com

First published, 2025

Paperback ISBN 978-1-0682140-0-4
Ebook ISBN 978-1-0682140-1-1

Based on 2022 BPhil thesis *"Toward an Epistemology of Aesthetic Intuitions"*
A catalogue record for this title is available from the British Library, the Library of Congress and the Senate House Library.

CONTENTS

We are drowning in information, while starving for wisdom.
E. O. Wilson

INTRODUCTION

*B*ullshit. *That's what the world is full of.* To your right, a large spot appears, growing and shrinking after a rhythm that is difficult to predict.

There is a modulated sound, like a record on a gramophone spinning, slowly and slowly. You are paralyzed by terror, because you are floating in an indistinct and colorless liquid where there is neither high nor low - the threatening spot could grab you, without you being able to avoid it.

Every now and then, a cloud of scent goes through you; in that brief moment, you are the cloud, there is no difference between you and the latter, just as there is no difference between you and the sound you heard - perhaps, not even between you and the spot.

Now the spot seems less disturbing, drawing closer against a musical background, a tune; curtains open and the soft object of your desires unexpectedly appears fully. No, this is not the beginning of a science fiction novel. It's a description of how a child sees reality, shortly before feeding. Too bad it's all false - just a beautiful story.

Storytelling is a distinctive, fundamental part of being human: stories make sense of the world around us. We think in stories, remember in stories, and turn just about everything we experience into a story, sometimes adjusting or omitting facts to make it fit. By now, after twenty-one centuries, if we can't tell about something, then it does not exist.[1]

Sooner or later, though, it's time to put glasses on, so as not to think that there is only what we can imagine, in the world and so as not to delude ourselves that there is everything humans create.

In the beginning, there is the world. Not everything is the same: here it is warm, there it is mother, there it is noise. Soon we begin to distinguish and recognize: heat again, mother again, another noise!

Nonetheless, all these things initially appear of the same coin: mere portions of the whole that is. Only with the passage of time does this all take on forms: the objects detach themselves from the background and acquire their own individuality; sensations acquire defined contours; noises change depending on the conditions around us.

We start doing and predicting: we begin to give names, to use verbs, to paint adjectives. This marvellous evolution of ours is a subject of study for psychologists and biologists, and possibly for sociologists.

But for the philosopher, this is above all source of a profound and even more mysterious ambiguity, frankly, of a millennial dilemma: are we learning to recognize the structure of the world or are we imposing a certain structure on the world? Is it reality that, little by little, reveals to us the mechanisms the nature is organised by, or are we the ones who organize the formless and continuous flow of our experience?

These are the two classic theses on the existence and nature of things: on the one hand, the realist philosophers, convinced that the world is structured into entities of various kinds, at various levels and that it is the task of philosophy to "bring to light" this structure; on the other, the anti-realists, convinced that a large part of the structure that we usually attribute to external reality resides, instead, in our head, in the complex system of concepts and categories that underlie our representation of experience, and our need to represent it. [2]

Built upon my critical thesis *"Toward an Epistemology of Aesthetic Intuitions"* at the University of London[3], this book is intended to map out the arguments between these disputing parties and laying the groundwork for a final, comprehensive answer to the problem. I will not provide full answers here, purposely. One must ask the right questions, first and set the bar higher as I do thereafter, before venturing into new models of reality.

1&2 Achille Virzi, *"The World in Focus: Stories of Hallucinations and Philosophical Myopia"*, 2010

| 1 |

The Art of Being

Representation, Value Judgment and Aesthetic Norms

What we know (knowledge) and how we should conduct ourselves (ethics) are the values human beings constantly seek and gain from every day life activities, cradle to grave.

Truth is what we aim for, by incessantly acquiring an overload of information (epistemic value), while virtue or principles of best conduct is our purpose for embedding the rights and wrongs (moral value), as we live together.

Based on the principle of the *Cogitatio natura universalis*, we are all born with the capacity to think; once that skill is actualized, we naturally want the truth or have a natural orientation towards the true. Truth, justification, knowledge and understanding are all forms of epistemic values or benefits of holding true beliefs.

Everything that acquires epistemic value is regarded as true; knowledge acquires a truth value and consequently, also our beliefs: ethical values or ideologies subsequently become indisputable. Nonetheless, the process of knowledge development is still void of transparency, firing up the bid among new epistemological programs.

Not by chance, philosophical aesthetics swings between a theory of knowledge and a theory of art, linking aesthetic experience to trivial grounds for any claims to knowledge of the world. These complexities expose the lack of a nuanced understanding of aesthetics that integrates both philosophical inquiry, and empirical research: an epistemological clarification of the aesthetics as a mode of knowledge, particularly in conditions of uncertainty.

Philosophers wild hunt, in any experience, the moment when the sensible intuition becomes aesthetic relevance (beauty) and arouses in the witness of the phenomena (propositions, actions, events, presentations) the alethic value, which then leads to the development of epistemic or moral values, accordingly.

Beauty historically bore the responsibility of portraying the highest values attainable by humans or generally speaking, the representation of truth: what we know, what is good and how we should conduct ourselves.

Ab initio, we find value in a — consciously or unconsciously — metaphysically conceived concept of beauty.

There is a denial of the epistemological credibility of aesthetic experience and value is generally taken to be subjective. The philosopher John McDowell has shown the importance of the aesthetic experience as a *barometer of value acquisition*; on this basis, the attribution we imbue an object (or phenomenon), be it epistemic or more dangerously, moral value, testifies to the constraints we deliberate by, everytime.

Schellekens argued for a reconceptualization of aesthetic experience as both epistemically motivating and inventive, suggesting that intellectual pursuits can be framed in aesthetic terms.

Granted, aesthetics makes something epistemic, however the interconnection of aesthetics and cognition cemented the idea that our understanding of phenomena is not merely a passive reception, rather an active, dynamic process molding our knowledge, and values.

Aesthetic experience always presents itself as a confrontation with value: an awareness of either epistemic or moral merit as something pleasing the mind (beautiful) residing in an object, which makes it "worth it" for us to come by, as put forward by Mcdowell, inter alia.

Representation [aesthetics or cosmetics] makes something true [epistemic], our will is creative [art] and connects to satisfy beauty [taste], shaping the existence of an object after acknowledgment (prescriptive): as Keats writes, "Beauty is truth, truth beauty".

Object-oriented ontologists and new materialists are booing loudly here, so let's make it clear, from the outset: if people don't [like] engage aesthetically, the object still exists independently but despite acknowledgment, phenomena may still be nothing for us (i.e. have no existential import) if we choose not to validate them, failing to meet all truth conditions (e.g. semantic) of any given theory of truth.

Epistemic value is always embraced with a belief that, if pursued, will lead to the achievement of knowledge (truth-conducive).

By ontological entailment, moral values are formed on the basis of *putative* epistemic values and serve as a guide for human behaviour (value judgment). In the making, the implication is contentious.

Epistemic and aesthetic values conflict when we over-rely on aesthetically enhancing beliefs: the true and the beautiful can pull us in different directions, forcing us to choose between flavours of normativity, as Zoe Zenkin put it.

Shusterman illuminated the tie-in between aesthetic experiences and practical implications, noting how the appreciation of beauty does influence moral development.

The puzzle cast doubt on whether aesthetic judgments should be informed by ethical considerations, thereby complicating the notion of aesthetic value as purely hedonistic or pleasure-based.

Each expression entails a representation. In philosophy, representation stands for both the content itself of the representation and the act of representing, that is to consciously perceive, in the context of *external sensitivity* (an object with its sensitive characteristics, for instance, a painting) but also to perceive, in the context of *internal sensitivity* (emotions, passions, fantasies, etc.). In the latter sense, representation is an activity of thought.

From language to art, aesthetic experience eventually takes on an epistemic meaning, passing from what is and what appears to be with sleight of hand.

Aesthetic representation usually refers to how art and beauty are depicted and interpreted, while value judgment pertains to the criteria we use to assess the worth of these representations.

In fact, generally speaking, art and beauty encompass all human activities of freewill expression (subject) and any phenomenon we experience in the world (object).

Art does not just refer to the various branches of creative activity, such as painting, music, literature, and dance, in the common sense but metaphysically, to any freewill expression or application of human creative skills, and imagination such as speaking, telling story, relaying information. Philosophically speaking, beauty refers to any presentation that catches our attention, and interest might as well be imageless (audible, factual, propositional). More on this, in the following section.

The philosophical problems of aesthetic representation and value judgment are deeply intertwined with ambiguous expression, our flawed human understanding and the contingencies of experience itself.

Expression refers to the phenomenological output of both objects and subjects, while representation pertains to how these are manifested in the expression itself. When truth meets taste, norms are in collision.

The interplay between expression and representation is single-handedly responsible to our understanding or misunderstanding of the true nature of reality - how x is presented as x^2, x_{+1}, y, xy and made to "look like" something else.

Determining the "true meaning" of an object or its value is an infamous challenge for people: whether any aesthetic value, in transfer, is objective or subjective a notorious meta-physical dilemma.

Historically, competitive philosophical theories have addressed the complexities of aesthetic understanding. Clive Bell's notion of "significant form" posited that the aesthetic value of an object lies in its formal qualities rather than its representational content, a view that has fathered multiple papers on the nature of phenomena.

Dominant contemporary aestheticians uphold that aesthetic value is response-dependent, meaning that it is contingent upon the responses of observers. Iosifyan set forth that the ability to engage in "mind reading" enhances aesthetic appreciation by allowing individuals to interpret complex emotional stimuli in objects.

The meaning of phenomena can be seen as a product of both the object's expression and the subject's interpretative engagement.

Philosophical traditions urged a more objective basis for aesthetic value, arguing that certain qualities in what we experience can elicit universal responses. For instance, Lopes treated how art experts identify aesthetic value based on their ability to track aesthetic pleasure, implying a possible level of objectivity in aesthetic judgment.

Unfortunately, the thesis beg the question on whether the judgments of experts can be generalized to broader audiences or not, predicating skepticism about the reliability of aesthetic testimony.

Further, the concept of aesthetic distance, as explored by Marin and Leder, proposed that the way we engage with art —through contemplation and emotional detachment—can significantly affect our aesthetic judgments.

The notion contaminates the whole relationship between representation and judgment, implying that any of our emotional responses to a phenomenon are not merely subjective but are influenced by cognitive processes that can magnify, and shape the true form of what appears.

One more stumbling block is the epistemological wall surrounding aesthetic testimony. While some thinkers postulated that one can gain aesthetic knowledge through the testimony of others, the widespread unreliability of latter took the wind out of its sail. Empirical studies predicate how individual differences in perception lead to divergent aesthetic judgments, thus suspending the validity of collective aesthetic standards.

Normativity weighed in with foundational criticism, as regards to the semantics, metaphysics and aesthetics of knowledge.

Prominent philosophical accounts of artistic forgery have uncovered a paramount aspect of the epistemic harm, aesthetic falsification ordinarily perpetrates.

Artwork reviews ignited epistemological investigations on authenticity and the value assigned by a subject to original phenomena (simulacra) versus their duplicates (simulations).

People often hold essentialist beliefs on the value of original artworks, perceiving forgeries as inherently inferior, despite their visual similarity to the originals. Essentialist theories brought about the bandwagon criteria we abuse to judge authenticity and the aesthetic value of an object, which in tandem, cause epistemic and moral investment.

Experimental philosophy of aesthetics opened new avenues for understanding aesthetic concepts, imagination and the ontology of aesthetics.

By examining how lookers engage with art in real-world contexts, experimental aesthetics perused into the cognitive and emotional processes underlying aesthetic appreciation.

Among the findings, if a forged artwork was indistinguishable from the original, it became hard to gauge whether the piece of art possessed the same aesthetic value or its worth was diminished by its lack of authentic provenance. The dilemma echoed in the work of Dutton, who argued that the history and context of an artwork play crucial roles in its evaluation.

To boot, the authentication process itself can be fraught with anthropocentric flaws. Techniques such as ion beam analysis and accelerator mass spectrometry have been tested to identify forgeries, stressing the importance of scientific methods in establishing authenticity.

That being available, the reliance on such technologies does not remove errors from human judgment in the authentication process.

If an artwork is authenticated solely through scientific means, it may lose the subjective, interpretative aspects that contribute to its meaning and critical value; a tension between empirical verification and subjective interpretation which is ongoing concern in the philosophy of art. More on the cosmetics of science, later.

To bring it home, the critical discourse on art is crucial in defining how authenticity is also misperceived in epistemology, since the true value of an object is often tied to its provenance and the representations surrounding it.

Aesthetic judgments can be influenced by the context where the phenomenon is and perceived, implying that the meaning derived from an object is not static, rather dynamic and context-dependent.

Such dynamic nature affects the general notion of authenticity, as the meaning attributed to an object (a nice car, a hot body, a belief in the truth of a fact) may shift based on its context and the subject's background information.

To clarify, background knowledge does not simply mean the reminiscence Plato first articulated in its theory of innatism - the *a priori* knowledge or intuition "in the back of our mind".

Equally, the term does not just refer to the previous data, putative beliefs or justifications we might carry over, as cultural heritage (and largely becoming *aesthetic impedimenta*) rather literally, background knowledge hereafter stands for the circumstances or situation prevailing, at a particular time or underlying a particular event for the subject: the aesthetic conditions that make experience, knowledge, or certain phenomena possible - informally, the *epistemic scene.*

Cosmetic tricks clearly resonate with contemporary arguments on how milieu, mass media and witness engagement frame aesthetic experiences or how representations feign epistemic value expression altogether.

The impact of contextual information on aesthetic judgments cannot be overlooked: background information significantly alter viewers' perceptions of aesthetic value.

Kanheman's study of human bias refreshed how the sense of an object is not only derived from its intrinsic qualities but also from the narratives and contexts surrounding it - before, during and after.

In the case of forgeries, the absence of an authentic narrative can lead to a distorted aesthetic experience; the value of any phenomenon is not solely determined by its immediate, physical attributes but is deeply rooted in the narratives, and histories that inform its existence like our storytelling around it, over time.

The contemporary landscape of aesthetics is bent by the whirlwind of digital representation, where the line between reality and fiction is completely blurred.

Everyone is a "brand" and the metaphysical corruption of aesthetic understanding becomes ever so evident to value theory, particularly in relation to epistemic values, since fake news.

In a tech-driven, post-truth era, expression and reception are the most affected.

Platforms like Instagram have altered the interaction between artists and audiences, influencing the characteristics of the most-liked things, often curated and presented in ways that prioritize engagement over intrinsic aesthetic qualities. The commodification of art in the digital age may exasperate superficial understanding of artistic value, where popularity overshadow deeper aesthetic or conceptual significance.

Bañez emphasized the importance of personal experiences in creating meaningful visual representations, suggesting that the subject's connection to an object inflates its expressive power.

Nevertheless, in a hyper-real society where representation can be manipulated and curated, the authenticity of this expression may be called into question. The tension between genuine aesthetic intent and the performative aspects of digital branding complicates what ultimately constitutes true aesthetic value.

Constructed epistemic values associated with distorted aesthetic appreciation gain momentum because of the prevalence of forgeries, echo chambers and digital reproductions.

The work of Huang et al. researched how the brain responds differently to authentic versus inauthentic artworks, studying the psychological implications of authenticity in aesthetic judgment.

Findings confirm that our understanding of art is not merely a cognitive exercise but is deeply attached to emotional, and psychological responses to authenticity. The implications for value theory are profound, disputing the criteria we use to assess the worth of phenomena in a world where aesthetic manipulation is ubiquitous.

Tayyebi worked out why the relationship between representation and aesthetic experience has become widely fashionable, especially in light of the capabilities offered by digital tools.

Tech advancements and evolution humbled the traditional frameworks of knowledge, put forward by influential rationalists, when the boundaries between original and reproduced phenomena became porous. Effects on epistemic value formation are flagrant and compel epistemologists to reconsider how theories of knowledge define, and evaluate authenticity.

The principle of value attribution assumes that people's assessment of an item's value is not always a reflection of its objective utility or quality, rather the subjective and sometimes arbitrary qualities attributed to it.

Walton asserted that the category in which we experience a work of art does influence the aesthetic properties we attribute to that work, in the end.

Music is rife with differences in the aesthetic value of experiences, because background knowledge (i.e. genres) radically shapes our appreciation of new musical works.

The kind of normative conflict that I am going to build up, beyond this point is one in which a single event p, which originates from within an individual, causes an increase in aesthetic value of

r (a mental attitude or action) but a decrease in epistemic value of r (or vice-versa).

Snowball effects of normative conflict have been skillfully discussed in epistemology (Siegel, 2017; McGrath, 2013) and ethics (Murdoch, 1970; Cowan 2015), but are relatively unexplored in the aesthetic domain (Stokes, 2014, Jenkin, 2018).

A complete theory of the norms concerning aesthetic experience is beyond the scope of this book but what is important to bear in mind, at the heart, is that normative conflict is the imperfect framework we (or the others) consciously succumb to, in the act, so as to make all experiences more valuable [real].

| 2 |

The Art of Transgression

Mind, Perceptual Discrimination and Experience

The concept of "being" has, inevitably, proved to be elusive and tendentious in the history of philosophy, let alone nowadays.

Modern approaches apply metaphysical angles to rule what there is (and what *trans*cends) and how we make sense out of phenomena: what is thought and what appears.

Epistemic distortion, particularly in the context of perception and sensory cognition, remains a significant concern in both neurosciences and philosophy of mind.

Despite advancements in our understanding of cognitive processes, metaphysical and logical factors contribute to the spread of epistemic distortion in aesthetic experiences, and unanimous judgments.

To be properly understood, value forgery must be seen in the context of our everyday, ongoing attempts to augment our understanding of phenomena, in conditions of uncertainty or for practical interests.

By applying artificial associations among epistemically genuine ascriptions and misrepresenting epistemic relationships by abusing logical wildcards, undetected aesthetic forgeries stunt or distort original epistemic value.

Men of intelligence notice more things and view them more carefully, but they [interpret] them; and to establish and substantiate their interpretation, they cannot refrain from altering the facts a little. They never present things just as they are but twist and disguise them to conform to the point of view from which they have seen them; and to gain credence for their opinion and make it attractive, they do not mind adding something of their own, or extending and amplifying.

– MICHEL DE MONTAIGNE, "OF CANNIBALS", ESSAIS (1595), TRANS. J. M. COHEN

From a neuroscientific basis, the brain's processing of sensory information is subject to various biases, limitations that fuel distorted perceptions.

For instance, Lahner et al. found out how the memorability of visual stimuli is linked to specific neural correlates, arguing that our cognitive architecture is designed to prioritize certain types of information over others.

Cherry picking can lead to a skewed taste of aesthetic experiences, as certain features of a phenomenon may be overemphasized, while others are neglected.

It follows that the way we perceive and evaluate phenomena is significantly affected by these neural mechanisms, resulting in willful or unwilling distortion of whatever phenomenon we perceive.

Montaigne held that no one has access to a view which is totally unbiased, that does not interpret by their own perspective. Precursors of constructivist philosophy, Schopenhauer characterized the world as the result of a tainted will and Nietzsche made perspectivism the *clean slate* of all phenomena, particularly moral prescriptions.

Nobel-winning psychologist Kanheman inadvertently scanned human psyche within an economical society to discover that only the underlying psychological biases of a person cast their own perspective as unbiased.

Later, Nastase pled for a rethinking of experimental control in cognitive neuroscience, maximizing the need for naturalistic paradigms to reflect real-world conditions. This recent call for ecological validity elevated the limitations of traditional experimental designs, which often fail to capture the complexities of human cognition in everyday contexts.

When aesthetic experiences are assessed in artificial settings, the resulting insights may not accurately reflect how individuals engage with art in their lived experiences, strengthening misunderstanding of the value in an object.

Mostly, uncertainty manifests itself through perception or disattention. While both rationalism and empiricism underestimate the authentic sense of perception, in its gnoseological role, as they treat it out of categories extrinsic to perception itself (categories extracted from reflection or experience), the ontological rehabilitation initiated by Merleau-Ponty and currently led by neuroscience defines perception as the primary experience of consciousness, the origin.

What I see, in perception, "is above all that the objects present themselves to me and that I am present to things, in a mutual implication, through that union with being, which is my body".

When, for instance, I am in the presence of a table lamp, I perceive not only one side (the light), which is in front of me but also what I cannot see from my angle (the darkness): perception implies, in a certain sense, a faith with respect to something I don't see.

My perception of the world is one among the many perceptions, it is never a foundation, a privileged position, rather a "reliable" evidence, whereby there is never distinction between the front or the back, the outside or the inside.

Paraeidolia is the well-documented tendency for perception to impose a meaningful interpretation on a nebulous stimulus, usually visual, so that one detects an object, pattern or meaning where there is none.

Notable example is the satellite photographs of a mesa in the Cydonian region of Mars, often cited as evidence of extraterrestrial habitation.

Ergo, the ambivalence and the enigmatic character of perception keep us hanging into the world, revealing that the world exists but in such a way as to be continually rethought, continually questioned.

On the other hand, while many scholars concord that attention and consciousness are distinct, it is popular to assume that attention is necessary for consciousness.

For instance, Dehaene assessed that without top-down attention, an event cannot be consciously perceived and remains in a preconscious state.

Intellectual history resists the Platonist expectation that an idea can be defined in the absence of the world.

However, what we perceive can be shaped by our minds, not just by the external world: intentionality and the mind to world *direction of fit* are predominant activities of the brain, making perception an active process.

Mental states are directed toward, or about, objects and states of affairs in the world, allowing us to represent things, properties or situations; people always look for a future state of the world to fit a current state of mind, adapting the object inside to match the world outside.

Intentionally or unintentionally, if your mind is full of assumptions, conclusions, and beliefs, it has no cognitive penetration and just repeats second-hand impressions.

In fact, much of what we know about the world like history, science and common sense, comes from the faith in the reports of others: testimony is a foundational part of our knowledge base we routinely rely on and plays a vital role in acquiring truth as much as myth.

Consumer psychologists have studied the heuristics that people use in numerical cognition to inform research on perception. Thomas & Morwitz discovered that the three heuristics that manifest in most everyday judgments and decisions are *anchoring, representativeness* and *availability.*

Anchoring involves relying too heavily on an initial piece of information, even if it's irrelevant. Representativeness involves judging the probability of something based on how similar it is to a stereotype or prototype.

Availability involves estimating the likelihood of an event, based on how easily examples of that event come to mind.

A witness may report a version of facts with the mistaken belief that is true - without bad faith - but due to an error in the process of perceiving, processing and verbalizing them. Unintentional false testimony in Court happens because the brain, during recollection, can process and reprocess memories in a distorted way, influenced by prejudices, expectations or suggestions, building on an incorrect memory that is then presented as the truth.

In *Languages of Art* (1968), Goodman described a theory of musical notation with the aim to show how well-constructed notation systems can distinguish valid performances of a work from garbled ones.

For Goodman, notational systems must fulfill five criteria. These include elements like *disjointness* (a symbol refers to one and only one type of thing) and *finite differentiation* (characters are distinct from one another, and it's possible to tell to which, if any character, a mark refers).

In natural language, disjointness and finite differentiation are impossible to spot, due to the inherent ambiguity and potential for distorting communication, and thought with the likes of

- vagueness (general terms, rhetoric, multiple meanings, multiple interpretations, unclear referents, comedy)
- culture (vocabulary, grammar, syntax, nonverbal cues)
- pragmatic functions (subtlety, formality, brevity)

In brief: context or lack thereof.

We are what we say and how we say it: the uncertainty we feel manifests itself through an implicit universal language, which each local language expresses in a different way.

Again, local must be intended philosophically, as particular or personal, rather than geographically, as relating to a restricted area in space.

Language is an indisputable basis for reason and in its partitions, and structures, the communication form reflects partitions and structures of ideas, thus becoming a privileged access to epistemic values, even if erratic, because each one of us think in our own language.

Riding this wave, linguistic determinism is a set of affiliate views whereby language and its structures limit, and determine human perception, thought processes such as categorization, memory and perception of phenomena.

Words, in relation to things are conventional, *ad placitum*, "by arbitrary decision" or *ex instituto*, "by custom".

With a deflationary approach, all that can be significantly said about p is exhausted by the account and the role of its expression p or the concept of p, in thought.

At the core, language is made of historicized and relativized formations that do not provide any substantive information or insight into the nature of truth.

Contextual influences play a crucial role in forming our perceptions and judgments. Willems and Peelen elaborated how context alters the neural basis of perception and language, that is, our understanding of aesthetic value is deeply embedded in the situational context.

Contextual dependency is epistemic dependency, since variations in aesthetic judgments, as different environments or social settings may evoke distinct interpretations of the same object.

The variability introduced by context underscores the challenges of achieving a stable epistemic foundation for aesthetic evaluation.

Habituation is a form of non-associative learning, that is, a positive ignorance not susceptible to contextual influences or formation of mis-associations between representation, and expression.

A vincible type of ignorance, this blank state of mind may be a "pure" direction to alethic pluralism but a featureless mind can be both empowering (free from normative conflict) and limiting, because the context ultimately commands the normative weight between aesthetic, and epistemic.

The concept of *habitus*, as developed by sociologist Pierre Bourdieu, exposed how habits become a "second nature", building our perceptions, judgments, and actions.

More often than not, habits turn our dogmatism into invincible, willful ignorance, such as is the case for a young adult raised in Islamist settings.

Nevertheless, while habits can become "automatic behaviour", they don't necessarily negate agency, because truth-bearers still need validation: recognition or affirmation that the person, their feelings or opinions are valid or worthwhile.

Despite the perplexity we face every time, language has been used, throughout the history, to create and pass on knowledge, validate values that exist within our head - and the contemporary society at large - thus both truth and falsehoods prescribe how we ought conduct ourselves.

Coelho, the latest opinion in a series, noticed that the embodiment of cognition brings out the interaction between biological mechanisms and cognitive processes.

From Cartesian dualism to modern kinds of monism, this well-known philosophical club endorse that our aesthetic experiences are not merely cognitive but are also grounded in our bodily interactions with the world.

The embodiment of cognition is a hotbed of aesthetic tricks, normative distortions in how we perceive and evaluate what stands before us, as our sensory experiences are influenced by both our physical presence and emotional states.

Epistemic shift in aesthetic understanding arises from a confluence of metaphysical and logical factors, including the loopholes of neural processing, contextual influences and the embodied nature of cognition.

Though neuroscience and contemporary philosophy of mind make headway, diagnosis of these accidental distortions rests without a definitive treatment, delaying the chance to achieve a clear and consistent theory of any aesthetic value, up and including derivatives such as epistemic and moral values.

Neuroscience is now the favored method for explaining almost every element of human behavior. At least since George H.W. Bush declared the 1990s the decade of the brain, the media have been flooded with simplistic empirical answers to many of life's questions.

Deena Skolnick Weisberg, a Temple University postdoctoral fellow in psychology, counterattacked in a 2008 paper titled *"The Seductive Allure of Neuroscience Explanations"* flagging how the language of neuroscience affected nonexperts' judgment, impressing them so much that they became convinced that illogical explanations actually made sense.

Similarly, combining neuroscience with, say, the study of art nowadays seemed to offer an instant sheen of credibility.

Of course, this is mostly a political bid to give more authority to liberal arts in the academic circles, disciplines that are more qualitative and thus are construed, as less desirable or powerful, in today's scientized and digitalized world - especially after Sokal affair in 1996 and the harsh Times obituary of the philosopher Jacques Derrida, in 2004, who was dubbed an "abstruse theorist".

Alva Noë is one of a new breed—part philosopher, part cognitive scientist, part neuroscientist—who is radically altering the study of consciousness.

In *Out of Our Heads*, he does away with the two hundred-year-old paradigm that places consciousness within the confines of the brain and argues that consciousness is something we do, rather than being something that happens inside us.

A thesis not particularly idiosyncratic, since Husserl and phenomenology but to all intents and purposes, field refreshing.

Reconciling idealism and realism by focusing on how subjective experiences inform our engagement with the objective world has been the goal of phenomenology, the only true and fittest theoretical contender to Kant's criticism, in the history of philosophy; not accidentally, jet-fuel of the current neuroscientific evolution.

One reason for the frequent refutation of Kant's critical philosophy and transcendental idealism lies in the protean nature of aesthetics.

In response to the demanding task posed by both Kantian and post-Kantian thoughts, multiple synthetic theories have turned up, in an effort to reconcile idealism, and realism coherently.

Those intellectual trends purported to bridge the gap between subjective experience and objective reality; the most influential may be generally grouped under four headings, in order of genesis: pragmatism, phenomenology, constructivism and critical realism.

Kant's assertion that our knowledge is limited to phenomena (the world as we experience it) and that we cannot know things-in-themselves (noumena) has been contested plenty by analysts who argue for the possibility of accessing objective truths, beyond sensory experiences.

Some philosophers, the latest being Burham in 2008, contend that Kant's strict separation between phenomena and noumena is overly rigid and does not account for the ways technology (and science) could soon generate data about the nature of reality, beyond immediate experience.

The development of theories in physics has demonstrated that our understanding of reality easily extends beyond Kant's proposed limits.

Progress in quantum gravity and relativity conceived new interpretations of reality that Kant's framework could not sufficiently address.

This empirical challenge to Kant's epistemological boundaries impugned the static view of knowledge, expanding upon existentialism and phenomenologists who were the first to notice how knowledge is not merely a passive reception of sensory data; actually, it is actively constructed through human experience, and relationship with the world - the dynamic give and take between subject & object.

When individuals or groups assert that their understanding of knowledge or morality is universally applicable, disregarding contextual and subjective factors, the rigid adherence to absolute truths or principles induces failure in recognizing the aesthetic complexities and nuances inherent in moral, and epistemic judgments.

The phenomenon of moral dumbfounding, as elaborated by Stanley et al., in 2019, brought to the fore how we may hold strong moral beliefs, without being able to articulate the reasoning behind them, taking a form of epistemic rigidity. Contemporary individuals tend to overgeneralize experiences and beliefs, resulting in an absolutist stance and a distorted view of truths as given, despite the lack of coherent justification or any epistemic ground.

Further, when we encounter differing views from those we consider equals, disagreement among peers begets cognitive dissonance that is resolved through an absolutist lens, for unity and practical purposes (pragmatism).

Unfortunately, emphasis on the practical consequences of judgments, and ideas tends to reinforce our belief that one's own framework is the only valid one, especially depending on who has epistemic authority. Ergo, judgments can vary significantly based on value aesthetics, yet absolutist perspectives tend to ignore this variability.

The role of personal commitments in shaping judgments is also under-explored in both absolutist and relativistic frameworks.

Aesthetic commitments significantly influence our [epistemic, social, moral and illogical] judgments. While ethical relativism and critical realism spread ground-breaking insights into the embodied nature of morality and knowledge, they eventually sold limitations.

In the chaos, critical theory offered us the fantasy that we have no control, making a fetish of haze, ambiguity and exhibiting what Alva Noë terms "an allergy to anything essentialist".

In neurohumanities, by contrast, we do have mastery and concrete, empirical ends, which has proved more appealing, even as (or perhaps because) it is highly reductive. Today, neuro-reductionism is the ultimate response to—and rejection of—critical theory.

There are things that neurosciences are useful for, in the matter of understanding behavior, but there are also things these disciplines are not all that useful for, like understanding the nuances of our reactions to poetry. That is not to say that all neurohumanities scholars are insensitive to nuance and ambiguity but "there's an attention to the fine grain of a text that neuroscience can't get at", as Jonathan Kramnick, a Rutgers University English professor reminded in his provocative essay "Against Literary Darwinism".

"Humanists are unwilling or unable to evaluate the science, so we just take scientists' word for it, without following up on the evidence or knowing these claims are highly contested within their community," quipped Todd Cronan, a professor of art history at Emory University. "Mirror neurons are highly debatable, yet art historians now just apply them to artworks. I think it's worrying.

And when there's a 'call for collaboration' between art scholars and neuroscientists, we just marshal the scientists' evidence".

Jennifer Ashton, an English professor at the University of Illinois, wrote a takedown of neuroaesthetics in the academic journal *Nonsite* in 2011. She put it like this: "How your brain is firing won't tell you if something is ironic, metaphorical or meaningful or if it is not".

Literary Darwinism is another route by which the language and analytical frame of science has entered the humanities.

Although neuroimaging may help us understand what our mind does when we read quickly or with a more careful attention, these data sets tell us next to nothing about the actual literature, nor do they give us a political understanding of a text.

Today, there's the sudden dominance of so many ways to quantify things that used to be amorphous and that we imagined were merely expressive or personal: Big Data, Facebook, ubiquitous surveillance, the growing use of pharmaceuticals to control our moods and minds.

In other words, neurohumanities is not just a change in how we see paintings or read nineteenth-century novels. It's a small part of the change in what we think it means to be human.

The apparent diversity of the modern disciplines is progressively revealed to overlay an original unitary philology, consisting in *comparison, knowledgeable interpretation*, and *sensitivity to context.*

I think that we are at a crossing in the roads of history, history in the grand sense. One road already appears clearly laid out, at least in its general orientation. That's the road of the loss of meaning, of the repetition of empty forms, of conformism, apathy, irresponsibility, and cynicism at the same time as it is that of the tightening grip of the capitalist imaginary of unlimited expansion of "rational mastery," pseudorational pseudomastery, of an unlimited expansion of consumption for the sake of consumption, that is to say, for nothing, and of a technoscience that has become autonomized along its path and that is evidently involved in the domination of this capitalist imaginary. The other road should be opened: it is not at all laid out. It can be opened only through a social and political awakening, a resurgence of the project of individual and collective autonomy, that is to say, of the will to freedom. This would require an awakening of the imagination and of the creative imaginary.

CORNELIUS CASTORIADIS

The concept of Chaos, as found in Ancient Greek cosmogony, connected to the idea of the "imaginary" plays a significant role in our decision-making. The feeling of agency, the sense that we are the authors of our thoughts and actions is the primary driver of our actions: consciousness is the foundation of free will.

Castoriadis translated the Greek word "chaos" as nothingness to purposely designate (1) the creative force of human thought in transforming intentionally what's on our mind into the real world - tangible out of intangible - and (2) our full autonomy in doing so, at any time, even when influenced by unconscious processes, said to be beyond our awareness.

Free will can be defined as the ability to do otherwise: brains can initiate new thoughts *ab initio*, independently of deterministic and/or indeterministic physics, via unknown mechanisms or dualism (libertarianism).

The facts can be staring you in the face, but your brain prevents you from seeing it. The act of making art is an act of freedom in itself and we make art everyday, every time we create something new, in any expression of individuality.

Human freedom to imagine, create and disseminate such as stubbornly finding (or not wanting to find) a solution to a problem is inherently artistic, aesthetic experience in turn generates new knowledge and all conscious or unconscious experience is fundamentally perception, interpretation and appreciation of the "beautiful".

Creativity, at its peak, is definitely the most novel-producing process people exhibit; innovation possesses the highest degree of unpredictability that certainly implies a randomness associated with human volition. That's as close to free will as there can be, if not actually free will.

Imagination allows you more options, which means you can make better decisions than less creative people but usually, the choice of taking a different action is not up to the individual representing.

In fact, the likes of Graham W. Boyd argue that choice is an illusion. The brain's Risk/Reward system makes our choices, not us. This emotion-scoring system uses neural pathways to weigh the-value of options, which can be modulated by factors like past experiences andemotional responses. Recent research shows the brain uses distinct neural groups to process both better-than-expected and worse-than-expected outcomes, helping to balance risk and reward in decision-making. External stimuli, including artificial rewards from things like drugs, gambling, social media and AI, can hijack these natural reward pathways.

The debate on autonomy in creation hinges on the idea that created things have a certain degree of independence: self-determination.

Hard determinists argue that all thoughts and actions, from common to creative people, are the result of prior causes (biological, psychological, environmental) and free will is an illusion: though we may feel free, our wills are actually determined by circumstances beyond our control. For instance, a fashion designer can be obligated to perform a task, by specific orders but allowed creativity in how to perform it.

If that is the case, creativity might be seen as just another product of deterministic processes in life, rather than the paragon of human free will.

Psychologists added that, on the whole, creativity is a social phenomenon, influenced by collaboration and cultural contexts. *Collective* creativity would imply that *individual* free will is less significant in the creative elaboration.

When you create art, you do exercise will but the business around will mould it and shape it, you can be obligated to perform a concert and allowed limited creativity in how to perform it: you may not have total creative control to decide both what you want to do and how - the core thesis driving independent artists.

Evaluation is an epistemic "business" married entirely to normative conflict, the aesthetic tension between ascriptions by our political self, and norms by the social politics.

In an era of increasingly advanced Artificial Intelligence (AI), where artificial representation abounds, people employ a rich tapestry of digital tools and "identities", which empower or constrain such individuality.

Digital identity replicates or attacks existing hierarchies: when algorithms filter what we see or who sees us, a transformative possibility emerges, yet prejudice may also be reinforced, since AI systems are only as unbiased as the data or engineer's model they are trained on.

Creative autonomy with AI in art is complex, involving concerns about originality, intellectual property and the nature of human creativity.

AI can generate visually impressive works, which in turn may generate appealing "alternative taste", generally speaking but it may not be "true" creativity, knowledge as humans make it, begging the question on why we nevertheless attribute value to them.

Hyperrealism is revived, developing metaphysical interpretations on the nature of human experience across business, art, philosophy and media studies. Broadly, the concept refers to a human state where the distinction between reality and representation is blurred, a condition where representations are perceived as more real than reality itself.

French philosopher Jean Baudrillard was a forerunner of hyperreality and first to articulate the implications of this phenomenon - the pervasive effects of current digital culture.

Blurring of external reality and artificial representation is ever so evident when media images and symbols saturate our perception of reality, to the extent that they become indistinguishable from actual experiences.

Epistemic distortion is rampant, because of professional-induced contexts such as advertising, social media and virtual environments, where the representation of reality is often enhanced or manipulated to create an illusion that feels more authentic than the original.

Baudrillard's concept of *simulacra* refers to copies or representations that no longer have an original or referent.

In the hyperreal era, simulacra dominate our understanding of reality, serving an axiological crisis where individuals engage with images, and symbols rather than the underlying truths they represent. Simulations create a sense of disconnection from genuine experiences, and values, surrendering nature to cosmetics - whatever ideology.

Paul Gaffney wrote a remarkable paper on Surrogates in 2004, aligning with my premise here that "not only do words have the capacity to signify something other than themselves, but also, and more interestingly, every aspect of Being, as well as Being itself, can play a surrogative role with respect to other aspects of Being" as in the case of systematic metaphysics "usefully explored by approaching its subject matter mediately - that is, sometimes we better understand A through not-A."

Implications of a superficial understanding of complex phenomena are devastating for society and culture, because individuals may prioritize sensationalized or idealized representations of events over factual accounts.

This trend embodies social media and NFTs, where curated images and narratives shape public perception, and influence behaviour, even when there is no value, at all.

Hyperrealism also elicits strong emotional responses and individuals may become deeply invested in representations that resonate with their own experiences or aspirations only. That's the customer of the future, who craves overpersonalization.

Emotional engagement can easily blur the lines between reality and representation, fostering a heightened sense of connection to the hyperreal. Postmodernism and largely theoretical offsprings across cultural criticism thrived here, despite a lack of convincing evidence.

The rise of social media platforms set up a hyperreal environment where users curate their lives as an evolving art project, through carefully crafted media.

Spectacles orientate unrealistic expectations, ideas and comparisons, as individuals engage with misrepresentations or cosmetic alterations of reality.

In addition, the development of virtual reality (VR) technologies has further contributed to surreal experiences, enabling users to immerse themselves in simulated environments that can feel more real than their everyday lives.

For the impact of such experiences on perceptions of reality and the influential role among interpersonal relationships, a throng of ethical dilemmas ensued.

Hyperrealism is prevalent in advertising and marketing, where the [practical interest] commercial purpose is pronounced: products are presented in idealized contexts to emphasize their desirability and taste.

Capitalizing on the disconnection between the marketed image and the actual product is not just misleading, as applied ethics shed a light on, in the last twenty years of cultural influence but most of all, epistemologically harmful for the consumers, who form expectations based on hyperreal representations rather than authentic experiences.

The effects stretch beyond shopping experience and pervade a country's table of values, individual beliefs, community activities, with a click.

In the realm of art, hyperrealism flourished in movements that intensify meticulous detail and lifelike representations, blending painting with photography.

In literature, hyperreal narratives exploited themes of simulation and reality to reflect the complexities of contemporary existence but music or motion pictures remain the most influential medium of our post-truth, high-tech society, after broadcast news, as corroborated by the hyper sexualization of entertainment products or the self-projection in luxury goods.

All in all, in the post-human, deep tech framework, the idea of autonomy appears contradictory, free will is mirage.

For developers, the sky is the limit but for AI systems, future is fixed: we can make rational, willed decisions but they aren't free.

Nevertheless, billions poured on the superficial analogy that we are robots, rather than puppets, as critical theorists fomented: robots with faulty programming and sometimes, with faulty designs.

In principle, we are said to be free from strings but in fact, we are not free to act against our programming, just like AI.

Such a position might seem to be entirely incompatible with the existentialist project, for it implies we can never transcend the causal chains that constrains us, and thus never really choose anything for ourselves: everything is chosen for us by relentless determinism, regardless of the delusional coping mechanisms we invent to pretend otherwise.

Yet, not every approach to self-creation necessarily involves free will. Nietzsche, for instance, rejected free will altogether as much as determinism. The whole debate, he thought, rests on an error: mistaking our descriptions of reality for reality itself.

The map–territory relation is the link between an object and a representation of that object, as in the association between a geographical territory and its map. Mistaking the map for the territory is a common logical fallacy that occurs when someone confuses the semantics of a term with what that represents.

Polish-American scientist and philosopher Alfred Korzybski explained that "the map is not the territory" and that "the word is not the thing", encapsulating the view that an abstraction derived from something or a reaction to it, is not the thing itself. Korzybski held that many people do confuse maps with territories, that is, people confuse conceptual models of reality with reality itself.

In medieval philosophy, essence relates to the defining characteristics that make a being what it is, while existence addresses whether that being actually exists in reality. Classical philosophy does not doubt that essence precedes existence, nonetheless, existentialists hold that existence does indeed precede essence - there is no predetermined nature.

Existentialist philosophers also acknowledged that our self-conscious, first-person existences face a number of constraints, namely we are embodied, replete with appetites and desires, and placed in particular histories and cultural contexts — we are, as the German philosopher Heidegger put it, *Being-in-the-world*, enmeshed in networks of meaning.

There is no human "nature", Sartre concluded, there is only a human condition: we exist as self-conscious, first-person perspectives constantly imagining and reimagining who we are, as we move through time.

Beauvoir, feminism and the Civil Rights Movement fought social conditioning, shedding predefined, self-limiting roles such as femininity or racial identity.

Their efforts divulged that although we are constrained by the mind, external world, and language we are born into, even if we are born into cultures of shared symbols and meanings that impinge on our first-person perspectives, we simultaneously have the will power to exceed, go beyond or transcend them with interpretivism, authenticity and nihilism.

We are ever-becoming, equipped with the ability to constantly create meaning for ourselves through our choices and actions - affirming, rejecting, or reworking the values. There is no divine will, no moral absolute, no natural law we might depend upon: we are responsible for ourselves.

By way of consequence, if we choose a drink for its taste, we beautify it over others; when we decide to verbalize our wildest dreams, we reify oblivion; when we choose to outlaw dissent, we dignify complacency.

Every choice we make in life affirms a particular value, at universal level.

Sartre went as far as to note that we are thus in fact "condemned" to be free, Kierkegaard shouted how our existential freedom leads to anxiety, because of the limitless possibilities available to us.

Given the anguish of responsibility, it is tempting to give in and fall back on identities and meanings already assigned to us, without much autonomy or critical thinking.

So, at the end of the day, art provides alienation from the weight of ordinary life, standing as the highest form of expression, where will is apotheosised.

Even when the freedom of our will is restricted by others, in ordinary situations or under the yoke of *deaestheticization*, nonetheless, art's persuasive form is the creative agent's ace in the hole.

The artist always shifts, shatters, dominates, with quiet explosion or subversion, in the most constrained of environments; broadly, an individual's formal recognition of the limitations of form ever dilutes its power of subversion.

All human creativity is embodied, based on "tagging" information and experiences through perceptions, sensations and emotions with meanings or actions. Our originality in creative output is defined by unique emotional depth, individual artistic vision or cultural context. No AI has these attributes.

Volitional control justifies full free will, present even when an action is initiated unconsciously, like pulling your hand away from a hot object (reflex) or unwillingly, like adhering to rules and regulations established by an external, governing body. Free will is quiet and subtle, and defence law shows everytime how tricky aesthetic judgments can be on epistemic possibility, to the benefit of our immediate, practical interests.

The absurd arises from the consciousness of a normative conflict between cornerstones of human life: that people care about competing ideals (the true, the good and the beautiful), that the true nature of things seems arbitrary (epistemically downgrading and aesthetically upgrading or vice versa) and universality does not concede "particular" concern. In Taleb's words, the core problem is how to live and act in a world we do not understand, building robustness to black swan events.

How do we deal, and solve the **absurd** in life or otherwise, how the mind sees what it chooses to see, is the quiz.

| 3 |

The Art of Confusion

Science, Epistemic Normativity and Forgery

Despite being a largely hypothetical philosophical enterprise, metaphysics has practical impact on science, information technology and society.

In the 21st century, distorted epistemic values precipitated significant ethical effects, check the realms of misinformation, populism, cultural homogenization and as discussed in the previous chapter, technological determinism.

Addressing the aesthetic tactics of distortion mandates a critical examination of metaphysical frameworks, calling for a more holistic understanding of aesthetic value in the transparency society or soon, the Imagination Age.

The process of value attribution to a phenomenon, both epistemic (knowledge) and moral (ethics), is constrained by multiple reasons, at both individual and social level. Philosophers have identified key sources and characteristics of these conditions, which bear down on how values are perceived, embedded and transmitted.

Through the transcendental idealism of objects (as appearance) and their form of appearance (ideas, values, attitudes), an epistemic value may be easily skewed by perception (and testimony) or by reason (and languages).

The main incidents contaminating testimony include social and personal influence, when "individual's attitudes, beliefs or behaviour are modified by the presence or action of others. Four areas of social influence are *conformity, compliance* and *obedience, minority.*

Group dynamics play the ringmaster role, regulating the belief to knowledge or morality. Implicit beliefs also concur as incidents, traces of previous experience that relate to the new representation of an object (implicit behavioral tendencies). Practical (or political) interests, though, are the most pernicious reasons of value transfiguration between people.

Confusion starts with persuasion, the act of inducing someone else to recognize the reality of a fact, the validity of an idea or to behave in a certain way.

"Practical interests" hereby symbolizes "circumstantial motivations" such as fear, pride, heuristics or any pragmatic advantage that may be gained by aesthetically deviating the original meaning in the representation of p or phenomenon.

Above all, the quality of interpersonal relationships does affect reasoning and value attribution. Holtz et al. identify positive relationships, comfort and group support as crucial for propositional ignorance or moral resilience, indicating that social dynamics either facilitate or hinder moral agency.

Institutional settings can impose restrictions on moral agency, pressuring how individuals perceive and act upon their values.

Deschenes figured that moral agents are influenced by historical circumstances and institutional systems motivate human powerlessness, subservience or factual ignorance. It follows that the environment where epistemic agents operate materially affect their epistemic or moral decision-making processes.

Further, the impact of social categories on reasoning is major constraint. Tullmann found out how social privilege can affect the understanding of others' mental states, pushing epistemic injustice and distortions in moral evaluations. This other element strengthened the notion that individuals' social identities power their capacity to attribute values accurately, based on diverse social contexts.

Cultural conceptions of morality prejudice how new values are understood and attributed. Vauclair concluded that cultural differences transform lay people's associations with moral character, determining that cultural skeletons often constrain pure evaluations and judgments. Cultural lens apply variations to meaning and colours in how values are appreciated by different societies.

External factors like societal norms and institutional policies, cap too individuals' ability to detect the original value of a phenomenon. For instance, people in a conversation may face practical pressures that conflict with their genuine beliefs or attention span, generating semantic distress: a highlight of the tension between truth values and external representation.

Internal conditioning such as fear, doubt, feelings of inadequacy considerably impact agency. Plenty of literature experimented that these soft reasons enhance moral paralysis, where individuals struggle to act in accordance with values, due to psychological barriers and the way these inhibit full understanding of the use, and meaning of normativity.

The embodiment of cognition is auteur-director of value attribution. Naeem discovered how cognitive mechanisms coax epistemic responsibility, thus the physical and emotional states of individuals do affect integration and subsequent representation of values. This perspective dignifies the union of mind and body in the course of any value attribution, whether it's a storyline or a given norm.

Cognitive integration epitomizes the teamwork between assorted cognitive processes in shaping knowledge and moral values.

Palermos opined that cognitive integration could be a model for detailing how beliefs are justified, upholding that the association of cognitive processes is paramount for coherent value attribution.

Individual psychological traits, such as personality and cognitive biases, freeze genuine value attribution too. Foster et al. defend moral distress arises when personal values conflict with professional responsibilities, pointing out that internal psychological friction hinders moral decision-making. Similarly, motivated reasoning can drive individuals to rationalize their epistemic beliefs in ways that distort actual evaluations.

The dynamic nature of values means that these attitudes can evolve, bound by context and experience. Brigandt documented that epistemic aims and values change over time, thus knowledge may be constructed and understood. This adds to our basket that value attribution is not static but is subject to ongoing negotiation, and reinterpretation.

Chameleonic reason ranks first in the list of weapons we submit to that aesthetically falsify or distort our understanding and change epistemic direction in the face of practical interests.

Rational agents would be able to think their way to a solution but especially in our times, in the crisis of narration, we learned how easy it is to reify a belief and/or reify its non-existence.

The coronavirus-related disinformation, which permeated social media and disappeared in favour of more recent news geopolitical agendas - the war in Ukraine or Gaza - urges to take skepticism seriously and therefore, a brief clarification of its collocation, possibility and actuality within a theory of knowledge.

Critics have contended that skepticism is an untenable view, both logically and humanly. Any attempt to formulate the position is self-refuting, for building upon at least some knowledge claims about what is supposed to be dubious.

When dogmas are beliefs accepted as true, it begs the question whether the principle of sufficient reason can be applied to axioms within a logical construction. Such intuition has exercised a revived fascination during human crisis, opening the way to what has turned out to be the inadequacy of foundationalist (or scientific empirical) epistemology as well as the exasperation of postmodern skepticism.

The vaunted human capacity for reason may have more to do with winning arguments than with thinking straight. Even after the evidence "for our beliefs has been totally refuted, we fail to make appropriate revisions in those beliefs," the researchers noted. In mathematics, the stable of possible epistemological strategies features:

- platonism (mathematics as an objective study of abstract reality, no more created by human thought than the galaxies)
- radical constructivism (with restriction upon logic, banning the proof by *reductio ad absurdum* and other limitations)
- formalism (whose focus is on consistency and manipulation of symbols, not necessarily any inherent meaning)

◦ logic and intuitionism (the constructive nature of mathematical objects, asserting that they are mental creations rather than objective entities).

Questions about the reliability and objectivity of intuition, for example, as a type of direct insight or understanding, and the lack of a clear causal connection between moral facts, and our perception of them constitute the fiber of its philosophical attacks.

As much as for the logician, choosing something to attribute value to, based on a whim or expediency, rather than any inherent characteristic is ordinary activity for individuals.

People decide, at particular and universal level, what experiences and signs in one's reality are one's reality, as we know it.

Reason is an adaptation to the hypersocial niche humans have evolved for themselves. Habits of mind resulting odd, goofy or just plain foolish from an "intellectualist" point of view prove shrewd when seen from a social "interactionist" perspective.

Today, cognitive scientists too believe that sociability is the key to how the human mind functions or, perhaps more pertinently, malfunctions.

We've been relying on one another's expertise ever since we figured out how to hunt together, which was probably a key development in our evolutionary history. One implication of the naturalness is that there's "no sharp boundary between one person's ideas and knowledge" and "those of other members" of the group.

That's why, facts are not enough, they don't change our mind, if we don't want to. Providing people with accurate information doesn't seem to help; they simply discount it.

Arbitrary reference in logic and mathematics is routine to understand how general statements about things come to exist, even when we don't know exactly which specific thing we are referring to.

Jumping to conclusions, also referred to as the inference-observation confusion, is a psychological term referring to a communication obstacle where one "judge[s] or decide[s] something without having all the facts; to reach unwarranted conclusions".

Often, a person will make a negative assumption when it is not fully supported by the facts - cognitive distortion is aesthetic.

In summary, beliefs are subject to our direct voluntary control and such voluntarism bears directly on what counts as reasons for believing, depending on how much is at stake, in the moment, for our goals, overall composing our competitive, territorial, artful, opportunistic position in the here and now - in three words, our political self.

Language is the representation of reason and therefore, by implication, carries on many political complications.

Handicaps here encompass the problem of universals, the ineffability of meaning, consequently linguistic vagueness and unclear references.

An ontology of universals shall clarify the relationship between language and reality, *Voces* and *Res*, thought and being.

From the antagonism between emotion and reason, it followed that universals were transcendental functions of the intellect: they exist but acquire meaning and significance only in application to empirical, and phenomenal reality (Kant).

Building on this view, the universal became rather praxis (Marxism, pragmatism) as the source of those meanings and values recognized by the human community.

In society, evidence is the condition of objectivity and when proved systematic, it conventionally qualifies as truth [consistency], made conditional upon the particular, rather than the universal.

More clearly, to be admissible, the evidence must always be relevant to the subject, making a fact more or less probable (probable cause) than it would be without it.

Human relevance or connection implies that evidence concocts with particular interests (or let's call it *situational risk*), at any one time, being inevitably mollified and tainted by the epistemic actors.

As a matter of fact, the weight of evidence in Courts is based on the believability or persuasiveness of evidence, rather than its certainty - reliability is a discretionary justification.

Since the concepts of evidence and certainty are elusive, truth is "the state of being the fact" and nowadays more than ever - in what Kincheloe forecast as "cyber-literacy power" - there is "a pragmatic subordination of information to practical action".

Evidence, at best, is reliability (or believability) and subject relevance.

Ergo, a skeptical argument does not imply self-contradictory knowledge of *non-knowledge*, rather an appeal to ignorance or personal interest outstanding in the moment, namely, a plausible assumption of evidence of absence or my own reference (what I provocatively call in mathematical satire, a skeptical axiom).

In light of this, skepticism is no longer self-refuting: we can postulate a belief about p's (total or partial) lack of knowledge, for instance state that vaccines are not good for kids but we can counterclaim the statement is legitimate, simultaneously, relying on a different system (arbitrary foundationalism), whereby the system is "everything you plan to create", as Schneider put it.

For every thinker and every time t, there is always at least one belief-system bt, which is available (at least in principle) to the thinker at t, such that bt minimizes expected disadvantage according to the probability function that rationality should be guiding the thinker at t if they had this belief-system bt at t.

The essential idea behind relational quantum mechanics is that different observers may give different accurate accounts of the same system.

Ipso facto, one shall not completely discriminate a skeptical or non-skeptical belief, as foundationless, for it all depends on the yardstick.

An "assertion" is something one claims to be true (belief expressive), an "axiom" is a statement everyone agrees to accept as true (knowledge illusion), in order to see what consequences ensue.

Until proven otherwise, my beliefs are all assumptions taken to be true, by my system, to serve as a premise or starting point for further reasoning and arguments. In other words, all beliefs, without falsification, are dogmas. All in all, basic beliefs are always "dependent on one's will" = they are discretionary and most of the time, we are unable to disprove of everything.

Science works this way, as the main source of human knowledge acquisition (and to some extent, morality) and the "arbitrary" proof in logic, statistics or the historical problem of method jointly give impetus to accusations of epistemological anarchism, as proposed by Paul Feyerabend in *"Against Method"*.

Mathematical statements are generally demonstrated by Implication, Contradiction, Contrapositive and Induction, which are *tautologies,* failing to verify the first Principle of Sufficient Reason, the basic axioms where all these methods start from, in their successful proof theories.

Numerosity is a distinctive trait of today's *Homo Economicus*: when an egg carton is opened, a set of three eggs is perceived, namely, a mathematical entity is suddenly realized in the physical world.

Taking the concept to the max, a problem for Aristotelian realism is what account to give of higher infinities, which may not be all materially realizable.

Calculation, the acquisition of knowledge through arithmetic and estimation - the process of finding an approximation - are not truth-bearing, just truth-conducive.

Mathematical finance models do not, for instance, incorporate complex elements of human psychology that are critical to modeling modern macroeconomic movements such as the self-fulfilling panic that motivates bank runs.

Skeptics primarily aim to avoid the acceptance of falsehoods but there is an ontological dislocation of skepticism, along these lines. Their aim, expresses valuation of the truth: the skeptics like logicians are investigators, not truth-bearers, as philosophers often maintain.

In the axiomatic vision of skepticism, expressions count as *non-inferential language,* the view that the skeptic like the mathematician does not make epistemological conclusions but only chronicles his own assertions.

Finally, the distinction between belief and skepticism no longer applies, as the latter becomes nothing but a dialectical characterization of the former.

The controversial stance follows: "a belief is the subjective requirement for knowledge, not the opposite" and until proven otherwise, my beliefs including skeptical ones are all assumptions taken to be true (or beyond reasonable doubt), according to my own system, even if it there is no origin.

A fact is a fact, just *of* consequence in determining the action or our belief. Even war itself has an ethics, controversially, founded on other basic deontological premises, completely discordant with most, basic moral or spiritual principles. Aesthetic norms are in a dogfight with epistemic ones.

There appear to be "no order of human life, or way we are, or human nature, that one can appeal to, in order to ultimately judge or evaluate between ways of life", that's why, Foucault insisted, for instance, on the need for continuing ethical enquiry, like judging a war, whilst lacking a universal system to appeal to.

Without undermining truth, reason or reducing the complexity of the modern world to a bad expression of power, ordinary people cannot help but notice how truth is absolute truth only to the extent that our beliefs allow it to be such, and primarily those of aesthetic kind.

Nevertheless, the quest for empirical certainty is incessant, with many AI researchers hoping that algorithms would be able to develop and improve our own decision-making. Unfortunately, artificial certainty has so far proved almost entirely illusory.

A typical example is the use of an "algorithm" to predict the chance that someone convicted of a crime will reoffend, drawing on data about their characteristics and those of the previous crime.

Statistical estimation crashes like an airplane when causal relationships are misspecified - fact correlation does not imply fact causation - or crucial variables are omitted or because models are purposely "over-fitted" to a limited set of data.

As with autonomous weapons, personal moral choices are made in the design and use of computer models. The more these choices are hidden behind a *veneer of objectivity*, the more likely they are to reinforce existing fake structures, fiction and inequalities.

Decisions nominally made by algorithms inevitably reflect the choices made by their designers, that is the particular again makes its way into universals like magic.

The superstitious reverence, whereby computer models were regarded when they first appeared, has been moderated: practitioners now understand that models provide a "useful" way of clarifying our assumptions and deriving their implications, but not a guaranteed path to truth. This makes a compelling case that rationalism, mathematical or scientific surrogates can obscure human agency but not replace it, especially when it comes to unreasonable human traits like emotions, rhetoric, humour and so on.

In constructivist-like scenarios, skepticism can never be total. Logic surprisingly empowers skepticism though, as it provides as much truth accountability as vulnerability through language.

I endorse too that living without beliefs is rationally impossible for us, hence there are established criteria for distinguishing falsehoods from truth we ought to embrace: sources, consensus and context, in umbrella terms.

Our knowledge is already intuitive, attained through standardized procedures, after which further doubt is unconventional, yet common.

The standards, though, are defined and produced by the same agents, thus it's still possible to ask, every morning, whether a given knowledge claim may turn out to be false, at the end of the day and that's why, the actuality of skepticism shall be embedded in an epistemically relevant form, meaning, an holistic, synthetic theory of human understanding must finally come up to unite the historical, multi-disciplinary branches of epistemology: the analytic rational right wing and continental irrational left wing to take flight as a society.

The Skeptical Framework is a potential three tiered approach for articulated objection, a table of reference to constantly measure skepticism in range, when criticism occurs, which is vicious both when deficient and when excessive. These we may call the "Probable Approach", the "Instrumental Approach" and the "Negligible Approach" respectively.

Every level has a collocation in regards to meta-ethical domains, in other words this is what may represent our gnoseological limits (or ordinary moderation) and whatever is attainable, on the other side of aesthetics.

Owing to this, skeptical phenomena get completely out of strict epistemological discourse and give us room to move on with a theory of knowledge that can finally unite the great branches of thought, reconciling scientific and humanistic, analytic and continental, easily.

From an interdisciplinary perspective, skepticism is treated as a problem to be solved but not all the problems can be solved, some can only be mitigated (factual agnosticism). Epistemic justification is not a necessity, rather a commodity. Instead of dismissing or solving skepticism, therefore, it's about time we philosophically acknowledged it, in a synthetic, dynamic epistemology, so as to bypass it pragmatically, just like we do everytime we use language.

Repraesentare is a Latin portmanteau, coined from a combination of the words re- (expressing intensive force) + praesentare: "to present, to portray, exhibit, to express again". As a matter of fact, phenomena express at first naturally and then, people represent them with aesthetic weight.

Attempting to explain all that, semi-realism was the last bastion of reconciliation between realism and idealism against confused knowledge, and distorted nature of reality.

The movement defends the interdependence of knowledge about objects (the *relata*) and the interaction between those objects, concluding that understanding one requires understanding the other.

Knowledge of objects and knowledge of their relations are inseparable, therefore the properties of a phenomenon cannot be "fully realized", without considering its relational context, within a broader framework.

The position is particularly relevant in discussions on structural realism and the foundations of scientific knowledge, coming up later but the problem of human awareness of internal, and external existence still enfeebles semi-realism.

On consciousness, panpsychism is to be dismissed for being reductive, mistaking affordances with substance and leaving behind the premise that the scientific picture of the world is still an inference to the best explanation - an arbitrary reference.

Subjecthood manifests consciousness unintelligibly, implying a distinction between being (existence) and being aware (consciousness), with the former attributed to non-human animals, by evolutionary degrees and organic complexity and the latter, to humans - the most highly integrated and evolved.

Drawing from Watlawick's and Friedemann Schulz's theories, value (epistemic or moral) is permeated by the Incidence of the Ego, which contaminates and models the objective sense-data with subjective incidences, in *transfer*, hand-me-down concept but relevant to reaffirm.

Aesthetic and epistemic considerations both shape and clash in our everyday understanding of the world.

Nevertheless, tainted will is a question of nature vs nurture: epistemological impenetrability is nurtured, I'm afraid; widespread are cases when knowledge (in its chain of epistemic values) is manipulated, altered and misrepresented, depending on how much and what is at stake, in that moment for the parties.

Aesthetic experiences might enhance justification, but their pursuit could lead to over-relying on aesthetically enhancing background beliefs that are not accurate.

Dangerously, aesthetic forgery changes the way we look at the facts, and the way we should look at them; it alters the scrutiny it is appropriate to apply, when attributing value.

Knowledge that one of the facts is fake only assigns the witness, "a role as training toward perceptual discrimination", rather than a presumed, distrustful attitude, toward misleading statements or misrepresentations.

Continuous quest for certainty means infinitism about justification, which, in turn still follows that the concept of knowledge is elusive.

And it's not the skeptic on duty to second factual relativism but analytical metaphysics with a series of epistemological experiments: (a) the discovery of double dissociations in the representation of shadows (correct shadows appearing incorrect, incorrect shadows appearing correct), (b) the formal study of holes or voids, and (c) the cognitive advantages of representational artifacts. Empirical confirmation is that every experience and language are transformed when they become the object of philosophical inquiry, and scientific formalization.

Metaphysicians turned the heat on the normative weight, which value should take precedence or whether there are circumstances where epistemic overrides the aesthetic.

Striving for perfect accuracy, sciences purport to create less aesthetically pleasing and more truth-conducive presentations of the world. Nonetheless, in scientific domains too, whilst making choices, epistemic politics is conspicuous: both the true and beautiful feud with our mind.

With this vantage point established, forged epistemic data allow distorted ethical absolutism greater leeway: bad ideas turn into group habits of no return, in less than five minutes.

| 4 |

The Art of Winning

*Language, Expression and
Interpretation*

The AI boom of the 2020s expedited the ubiquity of informa-tion. My focus so far has been value-based conception of normativity and epistemic dependence, events where one's knowledge, truth or justification for a belief relies on another agent, like testimony and society.

Non-epistemic dependence, on the other hand, briefed on how epistemic value is tied to other factors: the physical world or cognitive processes, that aren't themselves about knowledge, truth or justification, as these constraints just exist independently, regardless.

Across history, language has been used to build and pass on epistemic values that develop within our epoch, thus it also prescribes how we ought conduct ourselves.

Language is the necessary form of appearance of value (e.g. knowledge) in the sense that communications constitute the only form of expression of epistemic values (a picture, a sound, a sign or symbol).

This denomination is tied to the idea of "knowledge as a social category" rather than a material category, just like capitalism in institutionalized economics.

Epistemic value is a type of value attached to states of minds such as true beliefs, justified beliefs, knowledge, rationality or logical correctness and overall, understanding. These kinds of cognitive success do, of course, have practical benefits. One of the primary ways epistemic values translate into practice is at a macro level, by telling us how should we act and behave, what ought we do and say (ethics).

Epistemic values become norms when they are internalized as standards for belief and action, thence they have an impact on a micro level too, by making us independent and different (unorthodox beliefs), often alienated or estranged thereby. An epistemic value is one for which a person has reason to believe that if pursued, it will help toward the attainment of epistemic goals, in a wit, that faith qualifies as factual (truth value).

All other values are non-epistemic values, yet simply by pure accident, because no one's interest is at stake. If it were, one would adopt insofar as cunning and corruptive steps in reasoning or epistemological testimony - be it rhetoric or other linguistic expedients (non-verbal or communal) - in order to suit the meaning to the outstanding priorities.

In fact, short-term and long-term epistemic goals range from neutral interest in a random topic like asking questions on a friend's story they just told me at the bar, acknowledging news or information (vanilla understanding) to self-focused, epistemic agency of narratives associated with personal matters such as one's health and survival, professional standing, family and loved ones, social identity or practical risks (e.g. shame, falling, losing arguments or money), which may threat any of those, here and now. Across the board, the epistemic evolution might either serve or damage our persona (aesthetic self), our purpose (political self), thus forcing an ethical responsibility toward our Ego for self-preservation, where "the ends justify the [epistemic] means".

Cognitivist psychology and structural applied linguistics suggested that language learning is a conscious and deliberate iter of understanding, largely by employing grammatical rules. The theory contrasts with the audiolingual method, which focused on habit formation.

Nine out of ten, human knowledge (logic) alters in its expression (aesthetics) and representation becomes representativeness.

Linguistic analysis cast attention to communication risks and how language alters the ontology of values. The conveyance of aesthetic and epistemic reasons through ambiguous references, and vague linguistic expressions shepherd our misunderstandings (or misinterpretations).

A central dilemma in regard to ontology spins off existential commitments correlated to the use of logic: singular terms and existential quantifiers.

In the logical statements, a *there-is* sentence is the prime example of an existential commitment, an epistemic attitude expressing existence of a certain thing with "existential import", meaning people implicitly assume the existence of the objects being discussed and validate it, semantically.

Our lives are pervaded by commitments: you might be committed to meeting a friend for dinner, exercising four times per week, learning a language, being considerate, sustaining a friendship, promoting a political cause. Some commitments are relatively trivial and readily set aside. Others are deeper and more resistant to change: they persist through doubt and difficulty, giving shape to a person's life.

When people display extreme degrees of commitment, we sometimes describe them as devoted. Devotion seems to involve a particularly robust form of commitment, which might differ from standard forms of commitment in its intensity, stability, resistance to compromise, epistemic status, or deliberative weight.

Going from universal statement (generalization) to existential proof (existentialization) is alarmingly fast: by a constructive proof, as applied in mathematics, an object satisfies the "some" statement; by a non-constructive proof, there is an object without concretely being.

Existential clauses are contended between realists, who hold that logic is based on facts that have mind-independent existence, and anti-realists like conventionalists, who argue that the laws of logic are based on conventions governing the use of language. While it is deductive in logical analysis, the existential quantifier is not truth-preserving.

The contention that mathematics is the aesthetic combination of assumptions or a form of art gathered steam owing to the undetermined ontological status of mathematical objects. While the discipline is associated with science and logic, its aesthetic qualities and the creative process of proof-building motivate artistic parallels in epistemic domains.

Something becomes objective (as opposed to "subjective") as soon as we are convinced, ideally, that it exists, in the minds of others in the same form as it does in ours and that we can think about it, and discuss it together. Because the language of mathematics is so precise, it is preferably suited to defining concepts for which such a consensus exists.

Logical realism is rejected by anti-realists, who argue that logic does not describe an objective feature of reality. Anti-realism about logic often takes the form of conceptualism or psychologism, where the objects of logic consist in mental conceptions or the logical laws are identified with psychological laws. By-product is the theory that the laws of logic are not knowable *a priori*, as is often held, rather they are discovered through the methods of experimental inquiry.

A key tenet of psychologism is that logic is a sub-discipline of psychology, studying only the subset of laws corresponding to valid reasoning, as opposed to all laws of thought. Subject to this view, people learn about logical truths through the feeling of self-evidence, which is in turn assessed by broader psychology. Around the turn of the 20th century, objections to psychologism have been raised, especially in German philosophy, with the so-called "Psychologismus-Streit" debate.

The opposition insisted the laws of logic are known *a priori*, which is not true for the empirical rules adopted by psychology. Others maintained that psychological laws are usually vague, whereas logic is an exact science with clear norms.

Conventionalism is another form of anti-realism, where the logical truths depend on the meanings of the terms used, which consequently depend on linguistic conventions embedded by a group of agents.

For correlationism, knowledge is always relative to the overlap between thinking, and being - same space, and time.

Stressing the power of science, Meillassoux sifted through the "ancestral statements" that scientists make, such as the age of the Earth, to show the possibility of knowing things, independent of human experience: archaeologists and palaeontologists testify the existence of a fossil, its "reality" or "event", even if they have never seen it alive, lived before humanity and as such, before the phenomenal existed.

One major drawback of language is the ambiguity inherent in almost all human linguistic expressions. Words often carry multiple meanings, and their interpretation can vary significantly, based on the context. The ability of our words to refer to competing meanings is symptom of normative conflict between logical norms, and aesthetic norms.

Uncertainty triggers distortions in how epistemic values are conveyed, from the vagueness of knowledge generation and transmission to the subtle equivocation of what's taken to be true by society, as *nuntium, usus, ethos* and *historia*, in order of time.

History, unanimity, social impact, private/public exposure, minority influence top the list of normative factors.

A clear definition of "convention" is missing: customs are widely observed regularities but not every widely observed credo is a convention. Conventions include a certain normative factor that distinguishes right from wrong behaviour, whereas irregular behaviour is not automatically wrong.

Further, conventions are contingent, while logical truths are necessary. The discrepancy between contingency and necessity prevents the possibility of defining logical truth in terms of convention, unless a plausible explanation could be given on how contingent conventions ground necessary truths.

Latane's social impact theory outlined that three factors influence the extent we conform to group norms: personal importance, immediacy, and size.

The pressure to bend to normative influence increases for actions performed in public, whereas decreases for actions done in private.

It is possible for a vocal minority to stem the normative influence of a larger majority such as lobbies or LGBTQ+ communities showed.

Fashion choices are often swayed by normative social influence: to feel accepted by a particular crowd, men and women often dress similarly to individuals in their group. Fashion conformity promotes social cohesion within the group and can be a result of both conscious, and unconscious motivations.

Similar to fashion conformity, the male and the female views of the ideal role, and their respective body image are heavily affected by normative social influence (gender conformity).

Social media and marketing helped to portray what is commonly considered the current model of physical attractiveness, by the masses.

In 2020, self-representations on social media platforms like Instagram is interpreted in various ways, often leading to a superficial understanding of deeper political and social issues.

The aesthetic choices made in these "representations" edit the underlying values (truth, beauty, knowledge, moral principles), resulting in alteration of the original message.

Media phenomena like this are not new at all, in fact, the tension between the aesthetic presentation of information and the epistemic clarity of the values being expressed is older than the hills.

What's more, the intertwined tentacles of language and size of misperception complicate our true understanding of epistemic values.

Personality traits, such as agreeableness, influence aesthetic preferences: individual differences shape how values are perceived and communicated, therefore embedded by the public.

The way we express knowledge and values through language and aesthetics is not only a matter of content but is also deeply influenced by the subjective experiences of individuals. Epistemic distortion occurs every time the language used to describe aesthetic experiences fails to remark the complexity of subjective interpretations.

The role of context in colouring meaning is part and parcel of normative conflict, and denaturalization of truth.

Theories of contextualism in the philosophy of language explained that the meaning of expressions is heavily dependent on the context, wherein they are used. When values are communicated without sufficient contextual grounding, epistemic distortion escalates like a prairie fire.

To illustrate, the aesthetic experience of pain in art, as grasped by Ardizzi et al. in 2021, shows how the perception of emotional content can be influenced by the viewer's context, and prior experiences.

If the context is not adequately conveyed through language, the intended values may be misinterpreted or lost altogether.

On top of that, the embodiment of cognition concurs in how non-contextualized values are expressed and [mis]understood.

In 2016, Levin argued that the failure to integrate bodily experiences into our understanding of aesthetics neglects the expressive power of movement, and gestures. This oversight nurtures distorted understanding of values, as the richness of embodied experiences is often lost in purely linguistic expressions, in a bout of positivism. The aesthetic dimension of communication, nevertheless, is crucial in conveying values that are otherwise difficult to articulate through language alone.

Stanley Cavell made the case for the inherent emotional and expressive force of language, extending J. L. Austin's concept of performative utterance. He diagnosed that language is not just a tool for describing or performing actions but also a medium for expressing our emotions, desires, and deliberative influence. Those features heavily count in "getting" the aesthetics [full picture] of knowledge or meaning, particularly in situations of vulnerability and moral encounter.

The independent, dependent, and potential confounding variables are meticulously visualized and represented by statistics, logic and artificial intelligence but what can and cannot be represented by a variable, in a causal model is unsettled.

As discussed in the previous chapter, social sciences serve us the first host of problems, prompting to detail what sorts of causal variables make sense when we talk about causation, at large: how do we handle variables that are socially constructed (e.g. race, gender); what do we do with causal relationships that are contextual, as social causal claims often are.

The second host of problems arises when we investigate discovering causal relations from data. What's available in the data, what would be useful for a particular discipline, and what would yield models that are amenable to interventions?

The third host of problems stands out in formal work on causal modeling. What causal models are formally valid, and what do these constraints mean for causal theories? Interestingly, similar hard questions also arise in cognitive science: what variables are psychologically plausible and therefore can be exploited in cognitive representations?

The vast increase in data creation and knowledge dissemination coming from the 20th century innovation of Information Technologies transformed our knowledge society - creating and disseminating knowledge - into an information society - using the information to take effective action (always for a purpose or interest).

Although this can be beneficial for welfare, for instance universal access to education and democratizing elitist knowledge, big knots developed such as filtering, and data inaccuracy.

The very advancement of knowledge naturally creates the existence of increased ignorance or *non-knowledge*, however, the digital divide has tripled the roadblocks to achieving genuine knowledge.

Power (the ability to influence people or events, starting from small epistemic ones) consequently is commander in chief of knowledge generation/transmission and truth-making.

Once the practice was ascribed only to diffused means (the institutions, the propaganda); now it is joyfully, major individual agency by often one digital actor against the others.

From mass information, education, religion, politics to friends, family and culture, countless aesthetic tactics of communication forge epistemic absolutism, for interest: features become aesthetically relevant (epistemic desiderata), corrupt our perceptual discrimination and beguile us into granting epistemic value to mendacity, surrogates, replica, *non-things*.

These conclusions were anticipated by research on the political influence of media, a string of contemporary theories by social scientists and the rise of "alternative facts". Nowadays, social media and sensationalist journalism contain vast amounts of misinformation that mingles seamlessly with good information. Doctoring has been caught, the journalistic and political practice of shaping public perception of events or people, by exasperating certain aspects and downplaying others.

The constant bombardment of information, particularly on digital platforms has fermented post-aesthetic cosmetic epistemology, a distorted ethical absolutism, by bandwagon, where narratives are increasingly used for consumption (storyselling) rather than for creating shared meaning and community (storytelling). This shift, according to Byung-Chul Han, brought on a loss of temporal extension, an inability to construct meaningful narratives of the future, and a sense of fragmentation and meaninglessness.

One of the most elaborate theories of society fits like a glove:

> "Whatever we know about society, or indeed about the world in which we live, we know through the mass media. This is true not only for our knowledge of society but, more broadly, also for our knowledge of nature".
>
> **NIKLAS LUHMANN, *THE REALITY OF THE MASS MEDIA*, 2000**

Ambiguity, contextual conditions, vagueness and the embodiment of cognition thus cooperate to shift epistemic values at aesthetic level.

Based on a theoretical framework of neurodynamics that draws upon insights from chaos theory, Walter Jackson Freeman III established that the currency of our brains is primarily meaning, and only secondarily information.

At the core of normative conflict, the force of aesthetics is universal as much as personally resonant.

For instance, movies are magical, as reported by Cavell, because they embody myths, which inspire us to see our lives as worth living.

They restore our faith in ethical values like romantic love, individual autonomy, nonconformity, and the search for self-improvement.

We have art so that we shall not die of reality, said Friedrich Nietzsche: art suddenly changes the world, one person at a time and human condition is absurd, in Sartre's words, therefore we are instigated by our existential condition to adopt such attitude of revolt, words to actions.

New meanings come from the creative depths of the life force within each individual; ironically, the person is the last one who believes in their right to develop new meanings and people usually take everything they need uncritically, from the society at large.

Most of the times, meanings, instead of being free and open, are in fact "instinctivized" - hardened into the mood of a standard social pattern.

As we navigate these complexities and modern theories about representation, it may be spontaneous to defend a critical empiricism of knowledge, placing an emphasis on "being born ignorant, with all knowledge derived from experience - regardless of its authenticity - yet capable of continuously deconstructing and constructing to survive".

By talking about something, we begin to see things differently and, thus, make them different: reality is nothing more than the sum of the [past, present and future] ideas we have in our heads.

With words, linguistic intelligence and experience, we define the reality that surrounds us in multiple different ways, often modifying what we think, and feel about the life that happens to us.

At the mercy of this, Deleuze advocated for a more dynamic and fluid understanding of reality, electing difference as the productive force in ontology rather than repetition, the deviation from an original, unknown identity.

Intuitive knowledge and metaphysical speculation thereby become necessary complements to the limitations of our representational thought.

Speculative realism is a sterling move toward a more robust form of realism, within a philosophical landscape that [literally] lost the mind on the limits of human knowledge, and the primacy of the human-world relationship, for centuries.

Conflicts in value are the leitmotiv here, because aesthetic experiences can be appropriate or inappropriate to their objects, therefore epistemic judgments do not describe objective features of the world.

The value of a belief, and whether it counts as knowledge, truth or justification for either, is ultimately determined by how well the belief serves the epistemic goals of the person holding it.

Though I am surely failing to touch on everything in these passages, for lack of time and space, epistemic teleology, from John Rawls to Jason Stanley, is the original provocative view that "the good is prior to the right". For the sake of argument, and as immediate proof of our inherent Machiavellian tendency to what suits our self-interest, guess what: I believe that epistemological position is correct.

| 5 |

The Art of Believing

Politics, Aesthetic Decisionism and
Practical Interests

Aesthetic tactics of epistemic distortion are not just metaphysical and logical; human generation and transmission of values is very political.

Chief examples like an infodemic, when a prejudiced bill becomes law or generally speaking, representative democracies by nature, punctuate how a relative forged value may turn into distorted epistemological absolutism, effortlessly.

By vocabulary, politics refers to the social dynamics of power between two or more people when they engage, interact and make decisions (e.g. epistemic consensus, group behaviour and actions).

In a workplace setting, for instance, there will be a certain power dynamic between a manager and their team, heavily influencing corporate knowledge and ethics.

In my train of thought, politics is not merely intended as adjective relating to the government or public affairs of a country, nor simply to the ideas/strategies of a particular party or group in contemporary politics, rather pertaining to an ideology or set of beliefs by any subject getting or keeping epistemic power, within a particular social context (e.g. the liar, the ignorant, the skeptic, the egocentric, the humorist, the relativist etc.).

In 2012, Vogelstein analyzed moral normativity and how it relates to epistemic considerations, concluding that moral judgments can be influenced by the epistemic reasons that underlie them.

Epistemic reasons are typically understood as justifications for our beliefs that are grounded in evidence (evidential).

First of all, we know they are grounded only in the evidence "available at hand", not all the evidence at disposal.

Secondly, philosophers found out epistemic reasons have a normative force, because they guide individuals on what they ought to believe thereafter, thus shaping our moral judgements too.

Moral judgments are often seen as normative, because they prescribe how individuals ought to act (ethical references).

In 2009, Saunders emphasised the need for a normative theory of moral justification that would align with human psychology, urging that moral judgments must be rationally justified to hold normative weight.

However, rational justification is governed by aesthetic experience all over, as the way moral issues (or knowledge) are presented can affect how they are perceived and judged (or endorsed), eventually.

The concessions between cognitive and emotional responses in moral reasoning were supremely coded by Kennett and Fine, in 2018, while discussing the role of moral intuitions in shaping judgments.

With reference to cognitive and emotional engagement, aesthetic experiences evoke emotional responses that will influence moral reasoning too, showing how aesthetic reasons enhance the normative force of all types of value judgments.

Evidence-based justification, normative force and instrumental rationality are not the only properties of epistemic reasons. Gardiner added that norms can influence the justification of beliefs, that is, epistemic justification is not solely determined by evidence but can be affected by previously acquired moral considerations (moral encroachment).

A nun may be less inclined to judge the scientific consensus on gay affirmative psychotherapy positively, due to her Christian worldview, serving as moral compass in acquiring knowledge.

Value judgments are not made in a vacuum: both epistemic and moral judgments are influenced by socio-cultural norms.

Statements of fact (positive or descriptive statements), which are based upon reason and observation, and examined via the empirical method.

Statements of value (normative or prescriptive statements), which encompass ethics and aesthetics, and are studied via axiology.

The setting of evidential standards is often affected by non-epistemic values, as discussed by Elabbar, who recommended that the justification of evidential standards must appeal to broader values to make sense, such as justice, rather than personal beliefs (i.e. religious).

Olson's exploration of moral error theory, in 2017, put forward that moral judgments may be based on systematically false beliefs. This raises flags about the normative status of epistemic judgments when moral constraints are involved, as much as forged aesthetic reasons can produce or reinforce non-evidential epistemic reasons.

The fact-value distinction has been heavily criticized by philosophers and sociologists for leading to ethical relativism, where values are seen as entirely subjective and there is no objective basis for value judgments.

In truth, values are not entirely separate from facts, they both play a role in how we interpret and understand the world, however, valuation is a subjective exercise: the aesthetic upgrading (cosmetic) or downgrading process always affects the original value.

Valorization refers to the activity of increasing the value of something, whether it's a product, service, fact, information/data or even a concept.

In finance, valuation is the common operation of determining the value of a (potential) investment, asset or security.

In German, the general meaning of "Verwertung" is the productive use of a resource, and more specifically the use or application of something (an object, process or labour) so that it makes money, or generates value, with the connotation that the thing validates itself, proving its worth when earnings come about: a yield. Thus, an object is "valorised", if it has yielded its value, which could be use-value or exchange-value.

Similarly, within the epistemic sphere, agents choose to make an investment in the (aesthetic) value of epistemic reasons - to "buy into" into an information, a sentiment, a potential fact or ideal - and commit to the increase in the value of those personally selected "epistemic assets".

In economics, the value-form or form of value refers to the social form of tradeable things, as units of value, by analogy, applicable to epistemic, and ethical values as non-physical types.

Value is represented by the socially necessary labour time to produce it: at epistemic level, the time people take to create new insights, ideas, and understanding (knowledge, morality) through reason, analysis, and experience, and the act of sharing the findings or conclusions with others, ensuring its formalization and validation (aesthetics).

Knowledge is a product of labour, currently exhibiting all the characteristics required to meet the economical definition of a commodity: a use value (or utility); an exchange value, which is the proportion at which the information can be exchanged for others; aesthetics (an actual selling price, or an imputed ideal price), where price is face value (the apparent worth) and fungibility, for practical purposes (my word against your word).

Philosophers know very well that any product represents a value: the theory of value, like the concept of money prices, can be applied or linked to anything and everything, from the most abstract to the most specific phenomena, and so the talks about "value" can reach anywhere, with an unlimited range, depending on what one has in mind.

Playfully narrating the "metaphysical subtleties and theological niceties" of ordinary things when they become instruments of trade, just like knowledge or justification, Karl Marx provided a brief social morphology of value as such — what its substance really is, the forms that substance takes, and how its magnitude is determined or expressed.

The German philosopher mapped the evolution of the form of value, in the first instance by deciphering the meaning of the value-relationship that exists between two quantities of traded objects.

Marx then showed how, as the exchange process gets going, the value form generates the money-form - which facilitates trade, by providing standard units of exchange value. Lastly, he sketched how the trade of commodities for money brings on the investment capital.

The physical appearance or the price tag of a traded object may be directly observable, but the meaning of its social form (as an object of value) is not.

Objectivity is achievable to some extent, the concept of intrinsic value does exist, in economics but it's important to understand that it's a theoretical value rather than a real, tangible one.

The price of something is always determined by the level of interest (bids) in society - if there's no interest (taste) for it, there's no value (form).

Real prices and ideal prices is the distinction between actual prices paid for products, services, assets and labour (the net amount of money that actually changes hands), and computed prices which are not actually charged or paid in market trade, although they may facilitate trade.

Market economies often suffer from similar defects, in the sense that commercial price information is in practice deficient, false, distorted or inaccurate. This is not necessarily because trading parties intend to deceive - deception is bad for business reputations, at least in the long run - but simply because it is technically impossible to provide fully exact price information, so truthiness is accepted.

Market distortions, just like epistemic ones by individuals or groups, are events, decisions, or interventions taken by governments, companies, or other agents, often in order to influence the market.

Arbitrage in trading, the simultaneous different pricing of the same asset fundamentally confutes the law of identity, and excluded middle.

Much of the identity to an entity is being added by people who are arbitraging between the face value and the value added.

Price or the apparent worth of something is supposedly the intrinsic worth or worth an object or event has to a witness; value added specifically is the difference between the cost of producing something (the epistemic labour) and its existential import, effectively capturing how the worth of an object increases (or decreases) through aesthetics.

An agent increases the value by transforming inputs into a final product, marketing it at a higher price (value enhancement) than the cost of those original inputs. Market manipulation occurs when someone intentionally alters the supply or demand of an object to influence its truth.

In the context of markets, "perfect competition" means no single buyer or seller has the power to do such thing - rarely seen in its purest form in the real world but like arbitrage, it serves as a benchmark for analyzing epistemic behaviour without polarizing the topic to realism, and idealism.

Commodity fetishism, a concept too introduced by Karl Marx, describes the phenomenon whereby the social relationships involved in the production and exchange of knowledge (and morality) are obscured, and instead, the relationship between people is perceived as a relationship between things (commodities) and money.

As Moishe Postone clarified, the labour theory of value is not just an economical theory of the material wealth created by labour but is, in a parallel manner, understood as "human metabolism with nature" too, when looked at trans-historically: commodity, money, labour and political economy are not limited to describing the struggles around business, management and industry but extend to the way individuals constantly assign value, identify it and exchange it, every day, for specific, time-bound benefits.

The Latin root of the English word "assign" is "sign", implying subjects "add a symbol to" an object, function or process and on the strength of their mark (intentionality), they give the entity *identitas* (conventional representation) - the "state of being the same" or the characteristics that make something consistent (aesthetic), thus recognizable (epistemic).

Purposefully, French sociologist Jean Baudrillard proposed the theory of sign value as a philosophic and economic counterpart to the dichotomy of exchange-value vs use-value, which Marx and critical theorists like Postone painted as the modern socio-economical system.

Hyperreality, a concept explored by post-structuralism, describes a state where the difference between reality and its representations becomes blurred, potentially leading individuals to accept simulations or fabricated versions as more real than actual reality.

The law resulting from a calculation may be regarded as symbolizing (representing) one transaction, or many transactions at once, but the validity of this "price abstraction" all depends on whether the computational procedure and valuation method are accepted.

The use of ideal prices for the purpose of accounting, estimation and theorising has become so habitual and ingrained in modern society, that credibility is frequently confused with the real prices actually realised in trade (reality).

Creative accounting follows accounting practices according to laws and regulations but [literally] banks on loopholes, in truth standards, to falsely portray a better financial image of a company.

Hoping revived communism saved us from capitalism, contemporary society expedited a distorted view of value, where the social relations of production are hidden behind the apparent value of the object, becoming exactly the enemy many fought hard, during revolutionary socialism.

Aesthetic experiences serve as a bridge between epistemic and moral judgments, with pragmatic factors shaping value judgments and further complicating their normative status. Incoherent beliefs can serve as non-evidential reasons to fabricate judgment. Aesthetic reasons, which often reflect cultural and social dynamics, ultimately drive moral development by creating the context wherein moral values are transmitted and understood and always enhancing the normative impact of [enhanced] epistemic reasons.

Distorted aesthetic reasons breed distorted epistemic and moral normativity, dictating how values are perceived and acted upon, even when there is none, at all.

For Byung-Chul Han, it is only the mutual praxis of recognition borne by the ritualistic sharing of the "symbolic" between members of society that creates the footholds of objectivity, allowing us to make sense of something.

Exhausted by postmodernism's skepticism and dissatisfied with modernism's proud certainty, stranded by the shortfalls of both analytic and continental philosophies, we shall embrace a way of viewing the world with attention to misrepresentation, a metarealist philosophy that transcends and includes integrated pluralism, developed upon Russian literary scholar Epstein's namesake theory.

Indirect realism is insufficient, because the theory ultimately leads to skepticism about the nature and existence of the external world.

Post-analytic philosophy pigeonholed quasi-realism as a moderate form of relaxed realism, alternatively backing up meta-realism for accommodating different perspectives within a holistic, coherent framework.

In essence, metarealism aligns with critical realism, approving the reciprocity between structure and agency in shaping our perceptions of reality. However, while recognizing the dependency of truth on context, there are objective realities that can be discerned in the critical synthesis, as defined in 2023 by Houston, with dialectical critical realism.

In the same year, Kassel introduced the use of "epistemic ontologies", systems of categories representing our knowledge of the world, in developing a comprehensive architecture for understanding technical artefacts, and their material qualities.

By integrating realism and meta-theory, metarealism is an upgrade of indirect, metaphysically augmented critical realism, supplying a refined theory of how we build, and market meaning, influenced by the discriminant of aesthetics, without overindulging in *tabula rasa*.

We indirectly combine realistic and stylized depictions of the world, the external world exists independently of the mind, we perceive its objects empirically, then, we alter reality and style it to define it.

We not only represent what we perceive but we also augment it, for instance, when we apply the universal to a particular (e.g. chair to wood, dog to animal, emotion to a person) or assign moral value to an action: killing is wrong, though animals kill to survive; stealing is wrong, which we judge negatively only because we sit within an economical model, no longer the jungle.

The application of meta-realism is a laudable development in contemporary philosophical discourse to likely endorse, because multi-disciplinary speaking, these principles also address systemic inequalities, the biggest ambition of social constructivism.

Since Gettier, with some exceptions such as Timothy Williamson, epistemology has been encumbered by lacking authenticity, promoting analytical conformity and embodying a particular ethic of reasoning that sought to commodify the idea of justification, thus ultimately self-politics.

Knowledge attributions consequently take a practically-agnostic quaternary structure of the form: *"S knows that p rather than q, if and only if p is true for every case p is not q".*

People think that war is bad and not good but the belief is true if and only if "the war is bad" is true for every case "the war is bad" is not "the war is good". Justifications turn out true, in many cases but following the latter logic, truth must be truth in all metaphysical [mental] states too.

Epistemic value is an impression formed through the communication of information by the agent or by other value-bearers, rather than through the true account of the phenomena themselves.

Knowledge may be best defined as awareness or familiarity gained by impression of a fact or *situation mask*, where "familiaritas" is intended as "usus" or broadly speaking "conscientia", rather than "veritas".

Consciousness is not a sort of stage, a "scene" where "objects" that interpret images and representations play their part, appearing and disappearing in the backdrops. Representing does not mean internalizing something external to it in the conscience, rather it is an intentional interest of the conscience toward the real object, which at the same time is made non-existent, as nothing. The object represented by the conscious being is overwhelmed in its existence and made real only by its representation, thus should sensation and perception need the reality of the object to exist, this does not happen for the representations which, for the proven capacities of creativity and imagination of the human spirit, they can also exist in the absence of the object itself.

In other words, the reproduction of information or stories form the basis of the perception of knowledge by the majority.

Moving past the lengthy findings on why majority is always wrong, it is well known by historians that the naval hero Lord

Nelson often wrote his own versions of battles he was involved in, so that when he arrived home in England, he would receive a true hero's welcome.

In modern society, the press, blogs and other sources report their own views of reality, but in everyday life "knowledge as a style" may also be based on a political command, stakes or an inherent interest of the agent or the patients (personal politics) striving for agency in a discourse.

From Schopenhauer to constructivism, one can argue that the perception of all knowledge is created and in fact, does not reflect its true realistic qualities at all. Hence the historical function of belief in royal blood, for instance, as a proxy for belief in or analysis of effective governing skills. Such *impressionistic theory of knowledge* is a structural knowledge (*a priori* theory), where clarity of meaning and theme is subordinate to harmonic effects, characteristically using the subjective-tone scale (messenger), to capture a feeling or experience (impression) rather than to achieve accurate depiction (truth).

If you tell the story in a different way, then one can create a different reality: at epistemological level, reality is just a story, a *consensus*, what you choose to believe in.

Epistemic and moral reasons are normative for us, only when the socialised actor has aesthetic reasons for either, with respect to some proposition, phenomenon or action.

When the manipulative and hypocritical distribution of flawed beliefs and ideologies occurs (distorted absolutism), universalized perspectivism perpetuates inequalities, idols and malaise. Shining examples are globalization and the tyrannical Americanization of the world.

Usually aestheticism refers to the pure, sacrosanct character of the aesthetic sphere; as a doctrine, however, the concept is implicit in virtually all non-normative ethical or political theory, since the sophists.

Perhaps the best known formulation, avant le lettre, is Hobbes' dictum *"Auctoritas, non veritas, facet legem"*.

In its political form, decisionism implies that imperatives of efficacy outweigh any and every normative value: these aesthetically perverse imperatives determine "right", regardless of their conformity to moral principles or truth about "what is right".

Aesthetics is just a means of getting across your interests [politics] and worldview [interpretation]: form and experience over representation or function.

The aestheticization of politics was an idea first coined by critical theorist Walter Benjamin as being a key ingredient to fascist regimes.

Conflicts between moral and aesthetic value have a rich intellectual history, but conflicts between epistemic and aesthetic value have been less widely discussed. Background knowledge improves our aesthetic experience, and that aesthetic value in turn valorizes epistemic value (justification, knowledge, rationality, correctness, truth): all epistemic normativity is a by-product of aesthetic normativity.

Social problems of epistemic normativity and normative conflict supervene for the dominance principle, whereby the true and the beautiful pull us in different directions.

Aesthetically, I might believe everything in my work to be good, including the preface where I acknowledge potential errors. I believe each claim individually (epistemic rationality), but also know that some claims must be false (based on the preface, which is also believed). Someone's belief might be well-supported by evidence but clash with their existing ideas.

Choosing between ac-knowledging the new evidence or maintaining coherence with an existing aesthetic impression is a permanent type of human conflict.

Self-supporting and self-undermining beliefs attach no importance to facts, if people give evidential reasons no weight.

Our self is polemic, and political: the potential for individuals to prioritize their own dialectical (and practical) advancement (personalities, agendas) over the needs of others (and reality) can be easily compared to a political setting, due to the competitive personal and social maneuvers.

With his "Choice and Consequence" and "Micromotives and Macrobehaviour", Nobel Prize-winning economist Shelling introduced "egonomics", the view that people do not always adopt the individualist-utilitarian approach, rather wrestle with different goals and tastes, at different times. Unsurprisingly, an individual can make a rational choice, at first but in the end, does not act accordingly. For instance, some people know that smoking is detrimental to health but they cannot keep themselves from it, because an alternate self is in command.

Under the grip of aesthetic manufacturing, knowledge usually manifests in a inexplicable, oligarchic form, as opposed to a more appropriate, democratic configuration.

With techno feudalism, the conventionality and gross availability of knowledge has prompted to apply nominal value for practical purposes (easiness effect), rather than for autonomous purposes (critical thinking), thus promoting a digital, patient role, in society and political order.

What is true or false depends on what the facts are, from an authority (epistemic legitimacy), not on what we believe to be true, from evidence - the authority is primarily our ego.

The prevalence of post-truth narratives undermined trust in established knowledge systems, science and reasoning, creating a normative landscape where value judgements are contingent upon "political" grounds or allegiance, rather than actual "pure" standards.

The phenomenon of echo chambers, where individuals are exposed only to information that reinforces their existing beliefs, exacerbates cosmetic epistemology.

Daniel Kahneman and others have studied the psychology behind irrationality: cognitive biases disrupts the activity of value attribution, affecting how individuals interpret evidence and make judgments.

Mortals buy insurance and make other decisions, based on what comes readily to mind such as the previous recorded high-water mark for a flood, rarely considering that something worse is possible, and in many cases, likely.

The management policies of media outlets mess with availability cascades and feeding frenzies, especially in crime coverage.

"Strokes use almost twice as many deaths as all accidents combined" but 80% of respondents [in a survey] judged accidental death to be more likely; marketing masks the truth, because media coverage is itself biased toward novelty, and poignancy, to serve their practical interest of selling out. Yet the media do not just shape what the public is drawn to, but also are shaped by it, because mass media are founded and run by people.

The late Covid-19 fascination with death and populist interference with media editorial policies had catastrophic consequences for public policy.

Vincent Sacco and others flagged how the mainstream commercial media in the United States changed their editorial policies, in the 1970s, to focus more on the police blotter.

The human psychology behind *"if it bleeds, it leads"* triumphed and they would retain or even increase their audience, while reducing the cost of producing the news: investigative journalism is enormously expensive, especially if facts offend a major advertiser.

Focusing on crimes apparently committed by people without substantive political or economic power is cheap.

Some believe that the effect of the changing economic structure (or composition of industries within an economy) is related to the broader social change.

Vezér looked at the epistemology of climate change and its eclectic evidence and robustness analysis, indicating that social and political values can shape the interpretation of proof. Distorted social dynamics on epistemic norms and value judgments stand tall, consequently.

When information became the currency of our economy and we evolved into a *"liquid society"*, mass media, digital technologies and other mediated information took on a bigger role in our private life, leisure activities, social sphere, work, government affairs, education, art and many other (subtle) aspects.

The proliferation of social media platforms has transformed how individuals engage with cultural narratives, often prioritizing sensationalism over factual accuracy. In the post-truth environment, subjective experiences overshadow objective realities.

Taufik zeroed in on how new media strategies prioritize subjective values over factual reporting, raising a public increasingly swayed by emotional appeals than objective truths.

The art of rhetoric is a persuasive, multi-media tool for corrupting existence by persuading others (and ourselves) to accept a manipulated version of reality, often for ideological or personal gain.

Ethical values, in this scenario, align more with populist sentiments than with informed reasoning and citizens adopt distorted moral values that lack grounding in evidence-based knowledge or otherwise, constructive dialogue.

Economic theories of value have expanded their basins, especially in response to those epistemological complexities of the 21st century.

Traditional theories, such as classical and neoclassical economics, vouch for the role of supply and demand in determining value.

Notwithstanding, contemporary economic thought leaders sponsor the importance of social and environmental factors in value creation.

For instance, the rise of the circular economy underpins sustainability and resource efficiency, challenging the notion of value as merely monetary. An ideological move of this kind reflects a growing need for economic systems where long-term ecological health is foregrounded.

The integration of technology in economic practices has instigated the rise of digital currencies and decentralized finance, which redefined traditional concepts of value and exchange.

Watkins & Shelley, in 2012, already predicted how the impact of AI on labor markets and productivity would complicate our economic landscape, requiring a reevaluation of how value is generated and distributed.

Take a novelist featured at the front of a review journal: most people believe the critical acclaim is influence-free but actually hype is bought and paid for to generate demand (branding).

So, it's necessary to always ask about source of funding, because cash shapes how research is framed, interpreted and publicized, by now.

The study's results of a TV commercial may remarkably be favourable to the one company whose product was tested. Roughly 80% of AI industry studies are funded by undisclosed sources.

When studies like this mould public opinion, dictate investment and influence education policy, transparency isn't optional. We've seen this before: sugar (1950s), tobacco (1980s), Pharma, USAID (1990s - present). Each began by obscuring financial relationships with journalists, research and academics; each claimed science was on their side, until it wasn't.

Despite healing the wounds of the wars and totalitarianisms in the 20th century, democracy still appears fragile and vulnerable today, weakened by the shadows of aesthetic decisionism.

The radical about-face of global political and cultural discourse articulated by postcolonial, and feminist scholars who lobby for a more equitable distribution of power, and resources did not move the needle.

States and supranational bodies are a dialectical balance of democracy, law and authority. The political issue is that these three agents are all subject to normative limits:

1. the electoral system, which first of all circumscribes and distorts the popular vote (e.i. majoritarian system);
2. the non-democratic administrations and institutions that are part of every government, or the parts of the democratic state that are not governed by democratic mechanisms - these components are opposed to political power, the only true element that comes from democratic mechanisms;
3. the environment where democracy was born and evolved, namely the nation states, overcoming the peak of nationalism that occurred in the first half of the 20th century, are now gradually losing the almost absolute power that distinguished them, in favour of supranational organizations, and a globalized system;
4. consequently, the supranational organizations and global economic constraint, those who are not governed by demo-

cratic mechanisms yet increasingly influence the democracy of the nation states like European Union, NATO, ONU, to name but a few.

Catching cosm-ethics in act under the normativity microscope somewhat brings us back to Foucault's macroscopic theory of biopower, whereby the modern era is defined by the progression from the deductive state power of being able to take away the life or livelihood of citizens (practiced by absolute monarchies through taxation and capital punishment) to the productive state power practiced by liberal democracies through healthcare, and welfare to establish a state monopoly on the acts of granting life, meaning and health.

Byung-Chul Han undressed neoliberalism's use of new technologies to exert power over individuals by shaping their psyche.

The South Korean philosopher argued that this "psychopolitics" goes beyond traditional biopower, influencing individual consciousness and freedom through data capture, and psychological manipulation.

By political mimesis and obligation, popular sovereignty does nothing but fuel superrogation, evident in ethical and judicial particularism all over the world.

Justice is problematic, because it's the discretion of interpretation and justification, on a large scale - the paternalistic state writ large.

While the adversarial system is based on fair competition between the prosecution and the defense, the search for truth in proceedings requires a careful balance between respect for the rights of the defendant and the need to establish the facts. Adversarial techniques, such as questioning witnesses and the use of evidence, can be subject to manipulation and abuse, undermining the fairness and truthfulness of the process.

Epistemic competition between the parties is a central element of legal truth-making: manipulative questioning can easily induce a witness to provide false answers. Social distortions of normative judgment penetrate deeply because of the judiciary.

Democracy is not static, perfect, as most believe but like other social dynamics is a concept in continuous evolution and major contributor to normative conflict, at higher levels.

Journalists shall broaden the scope of their economic-political analyses, not always and only reduce the responsibilities to the individual, like the trend of vulgar anti-capitalism that seeks obsessive personification of all elements of *laissez-faire*.

Though every democratic system has introduced control bodies to prevent the political majority from gaining absolute control, those mechanisms risk slowing down, in the ordinary exercise of decision-making, generating in turn, the crisis of the value system and suddenly leaving universality prey to particular values.

Political, and judicial systems suffer normative conflict and epitomize the large-scale effects of value distortion, igniting false absolutisms with basis to epistemic void.

| 6 |

The Art of Mistaking

Ethics, Deaestheticization and Normative Conflict

L aw outshines the many aspects of human experience dominat-
ing philosophical reflection, since ancient times.

Philosophy of law and pure philosophy can never go unpaired,
because the political connection between knowledge, language
and power is intense: it corresponds to the ontological status of
values in society, where our sense of morality - our ability to separate right from wrong - emerges from. Let's detour for a minute.

The reliability of moral intuitions [case judgments] changes
upon our "reflective equilibrium", conveying a deliberative socio-
political constraint on normativity.

At prima facie, the choices made in a social position constitute
a strong normative justification for the principles of justice, yet
still merely political.

These are totally arbitrary, can be characterized by Kantianism but lack the individual characteristics of human beings, since the social interests do not allow to take into consideration human aspects like preferences, attitudes, needs and the biographical characterizations of people.

Furthermore, outside the systemic position of subordination, the problem of the motivation that drives individuals in social moral choices persists, in the sense that they are now real subjects, with their set of beliefs, aspirations and it becomes essential they find real and not imposed motivations to follow the principles of justice.

To bridge the gap, we employ a personal justificatory moment (reflexive equilibrium) whose condition is not that of unforced human beings, rather people in sociality, in a context of pluralism and cooperation: here we take the principles of justice derived from the political choices, at social peaks and to these, we add human aspects: beliefs, interests, conception of a good life.

Thus, this is a moment of reflection and personal deliberation, whereby reasoning kicks off from premises, constituted by the standardized principles of justice and opinions on human, moral, ethical, and religious questions.

We can easily speak of *actualization of the choices* made in an abstract position toward a real social context.

Our reflective balance makes it possible to adapt the constructed principles of justice (whose strong normative characteristics seem insurmountable) to the issues of the world, modeling them over time on the basis of historical and social evolution.

The immersive nature of self-as-object processing is manifest in the way we typically do not regard our thoughts as just thoughts, we do not recognize how perceptions and beliefs are just a model - working hypothesis about reality rather than reality itself.

On the contrary, we implicitly or explicitly take this mental activity to reflect reality - more or less - accurately.

People are incontrovertibly egocentric, self-relevant information is preferentially processed and remembered, and people strive to protect their self-views to the point that they selectively seek confirmatory evidence, otherwise reality aesthetically shifts.

Consequently, there is a moral and epistemic problem regarding the genetics of principles, which by their nature respond to strong constraints: universality, generality, publicity, finality and ordering in conflicting claims; these are conditions that make it possible to uniquely define the objectivity of a moral principle but in reflective equilibrium, are constantly and individually revisited.

Case judgments hail from the standpoint of individuals and try to find a coherence with the general principles of justice, which do not change in their substance but in their interpretation, in a context where human beings make decisions knowing who they are.

Bounded rationality is the idea that rationality is limited when individuals make decisions, and under these limitations, rational individuals will select a decision that is satisfactory rather than optimal.

Limitations include the difficulty of the problem requiring a decision, the cognitive capability of the mind, and the time available to make the decision. Decision-makers, from this perspective, act as satisfiers, seeking a satisfactory solution, with everything that they have at the moment rather than an optimal solution.

Therefore, humans do not undertake a full cost-benefit analysis to determine the optimal decision, but rather, choose an option that fulfills their adequacy criteria.

Continually changing, language is a critical factor of normative conflict.

When an abstract concept becomes ambiguous (or perhaps always was), the idea enjoys self-reinforcing function from the subject. Ambiguity creates confusion, chatter, engagement: natural surfacing, therefore takes on an influential role in the moment, discourse, action pattern or causality event chain.

It may as well be adaptable, permitting subtle *non sequiturs*, like when we don't have time to explain or purposely retell a story differently, still making its way in the influential sphere. Something we hear, see or do may also not feel ambiguous, rather evocative: feels like it should cohere, it is difficult to thwart and usually, it's institutional, still very influential for us, there and then.

Over time, popularity increases ("if it's popular, there's gotta be something to it") and the count of captured experts increases too ("if so many smart people integrate it, there's gotta be something to it").

Wildcards in programming, such as the asterisk (*) or question mark (?), allow you to match patterns in strings or File names without specifying the exact characters. Depending on the wildcard's behavior, a character or pattern might represent one or more characters or segments - a range of possibilities - enabling flexibility in matching data.

It looks like people do the same, everyday, in epistemic operations, creating flexible regular expressions of knowledge. Wildcards are extremely useful. They can turn weak hands into kingmakers. They can turn low pairs into royal flushes.

Their power is that they don't mean anything discrete and coherent unless, and until they're integrated into a final, optimal hand resolution.

There is an analogous object, with analogous utility, in logic and rhetoric. Any claim that has no discrete and articulable truth value can qualify, and there are many ways that a claim can be "amorphous", in this manner.

If any of these problems are present and yet are undetected, and treated like coherent and solid claims with discernible truth values, they can mutate and solidify around whatever the hand-holder desires.

Logical wildcards can take on a life of their own: their power compounds as they turn heuristics we depend upon (popularity & experts) into carriers by "capturing" them.

Nevertheless, beyond bias and reasoning errors in moral psychology, our intellectual romance for constructivism is not all troublesome.

Storytelling, artistic creation and innovation are just some of the most marvellous effects of how our will (art) alters knowledge, morality (value) in expression (form or representation).

Art creates reality, in a certain way: what Isaac Asimov's hard fiction books humored us few decades earlier, it is now a world possibility driving technological evolution. More so, art, science, and other creative endeavors valorize reality, when wood takes the meaning of chair, space takes the meaning of land, time takes the meaning of age, and so forth.

Even if the contribution of the avant-garde might be classified as paradoxical, the development of the "society of the creativity" points toward a central paradox within the free will in creativity itself.

As Reckwitz correctly notes anticipating the AI-enhanced creatives, "the once elitist and oppositional programme of creativity has finally become desirable for all and at the same time, unfortunately, obligatory for all".

This development goes fundamentally hand in hand with what Adorno, in a 1953 essay on jazz, termed *deaestheticization*, whose original can be traced to the industrialisation of culture and as such, can be interpreted as the opposite of creativity, rather with a "democratic" deastheticization whose horizons remained the communist ideals of many.

In Mouffe's terms, with the transition of art into everyday life a *deaestheticization* takes place: the deaestheticization of art is a response to the increasingly exacerbated aestheticization of products.

Among these products, knowledge and morality stand out miserably as top sellers. If objects had an intrinsic value, then money wouldn't be a conduit but everything has a price: a collective projection we all agreed on, like the currency of language, thus value added would suffice.

Economics validates every week how the value of something can exist simultaneously as an objective and subjective phenomenon, and that value can change quickly in swift circumstances.

A striking example is the so-called monetary seigniorage, when the governments purchase real resources (the goods and services that make up public spending, interest and fees from the loans they provide to banks) with zero resources (the economic value of paper money) for money creation.

Silvio Gesell denied value theory in economics, for being useless and preventing economics from becoming science.

Notwithstanding, a theory of value does make desperate sense, when considering social issues of interpretation, the "commodification of knowledge" and all in all, the difficulties of value-form, namely ideologization.

In 20th-century discussions of Karl Marx's economics, the transformation problem is the paradox of finding a general rule to transform the "values" of commodities by, into the "competitive prices" of the marketplace.

Marx's labor theory of value suggested that commodity prices should reflect labor time, but the observed prices of production actually don't.

The utility theory of value was the belief that price and value were solely based on how much "use" an individual received from a commodity. However, this theory is rejected since Smith's *The Wealth of Nations:* the famous diamond–water paradox dismantles its tenets, by examining the use in comparison to price of these goods. Water, while necessary for life, is far less expensive than diamonds, which have basically no use.

In the post-scarcity economy, the idea that profit is derived from the exploitation of labor is outdated but catalytic in understanding how the idea of "everywhere, anything of value" is gaining traction as the world moves towards a future where [value is subjective] any asset, whether tangible or intangible, can be tokenised and traded as a new store of value, further blurring the lines between the perceived utility (demand) of an object and its representation (supply).

At its core, arbitrage violates the law of one price, a situation when you and I have different constraints or preferences, and someone can exploit this. It happens the same in the market of truth, everyday.

Contractualism bases the structures of its value theory on a *consensus abstraction*: always and in any case, an enforcement of abstract concepts to human cases, almost never repeatable, in time and space.

Morality is a construct, culturally and politically relative, yet its universalization is necessary for practice and *symbiosis*.

Ethics is the standard of what is right and wrong, and they are based on epistemic values, even when these are arbitrary and manufactured.

Each political order incorporates in its own system a purely oligarchic and relative vision of good and evil, elevating it to conventions and constructed universal norms (e.g. taxation, deontology, customary law) to force individuals to obey.

The theory of the efficacy of a justice system vows law to be a positive social technique, and the only possible law. Per legal positivism, the legislator achieves or attempts to achieve its desired welfare state, by attaching a specific coercive act of the State to the human behaviour viewed by the latter, as socially harmful. With the threat of such coercive power, perceived by citizens as an evil to be avoided, the legal system aims to induce nationals to pursue the opposite conduct, that is, the one desired at the top.

Moral rules and social institutions evidence an astonishing cultural and historical variability: ethics is learned, in the context of particular cultures, and the power in the principles is deeply tied to the way in which they are represented.

Beliefs – values, attitudes, judgments, and ideologies – are reciprocally influenced by our social structure, as well as how and when these constructs dictate situated behaviour, in everyday life, prominently moral judgments in contemporary bio-ethical issues.

Grasping the dangerous relations between language, knowledge and power, we recognize the tendency of post-truth social value systems to create modern myths.

The term *"ethical personalization"* may be applied to describe the political tendency of any social system to privatize moral responsibility to each member of society, making individuals liable for a mythological order through abnegation and coercion.

The contemporary erosion of trust in institutions and the rise of misinformation necessitate a deep inquiry into how collective memory is constructed and manipulated, particularly in relation to history, politics, and identity (e.g. Gaza through whose lens?).

Contemporary society, at the apex of human achievements, has also achieved the highest level of *existential toxicity*, undergirded by the Digital Revolution.

We shall fault (1) the absolutes of men (or humankind's existential defense mechanisms) and (2) the false values (constructed social goods and evils alienating the fabric of society).

Value pluralism is the driving force of existential crisis and po-larisation of post-modern society, in response to the swamping problems out of monistic accounts of value.

As regards the beauty, our aesthetic preference has rapidly compressed, while "being perfect" became an ethical ideal to live by, which goes to show how epistemic attitudes become habits of conduct (epistemology is ethics). Tricks like this are ascribable triggers of body size distortions, dysfunctional social dynamics and mental health decline.

Secondly, the measure of *good*, paramount as honour or piety until recent times, has now faded in importance and radically transformed, at the outset of the 21st century.

For a person to be good, nowadays, they ought to be utile (or *smart*), rather than virtuous; even if that implies being cunning, brazen and opportunistic, by having no regard for anybody or criminal law.

Such ethical distortion is the main trigger, instead, of youth crime progress, of financial corruption and of a *quiet* criminal presence, in Western countries, whose political landscapes are dotted with common clichés of local-regional civic nature.

In the current state of affairs, happiness is the closest thing we have to a *summum bonum* - the highest good - all other goods flow from.

In a nutshell, an individual is worth for what they earn, and the gain is linked to the success they display (persona).

Maximising pleasure is the modern view of happiness, meeting the standard set by Epicurean or utilitarian views, yet it is mis-taken, for pain is an inevitable consequence of being alive.

As Nietzsche noted, a life of meaningful pain might be more valuable than a life of meaningless pleasure; the passing pleasure of happiness is secondary to living a good life, of achieving what Aristotle called *eudaemonia* - a distinctive contrast to our modern conception of happiness. By misunderstanding happiness, the distorted "value" of goodness fast-tracked the likelihood of disappointment we regularly witness with increasingly lethargic youth, and passive lifestyles.

Thirdly, we suffer a constructed and failed value of truth, consistently displaying inability to discern fact from fiction - what Hannah Arendt called *defactualization*. Transforming information and epistemic values is at its peak, in public and private contexts, blurring the line between "fact and fantasy".

Objective facts are less influential in shaping public opinion than personal beliefs and emotions, a contemporary cultural and political condition rightly known as "post-truth".

Resuming the earlier philosophical analysis on aesthetic experience and cosmetic epistemology, there is an over-reliance on subjective narratives over empirical evidence and the biggest challenge lies in upholding universal values, if any, amidst a landscape where personal often overshadow objective values, while non-valuable phenomena are perceived as values and acted upon in society, without casting a doubt.

The *existential pollution* is mostly apparent, as expressed by capitalism: consumerism, its core ideology, has generated an abundance of material possessions or resources, exasperating practical interests, rather than promoting epistemic (or moral) concerns.

This is proportionally direct to the progress of concrete social evils such as migration, overpopulation, poverty, discrimination, racism, sexism (including homophobia and transphobia, of which they are derivative), crime and drugs use, and this risk package exacerbated inequality.

On a closer look, the main drivers resulted to be: (1) the inefficient income distribution of public finance, impacting key areas for social elevation across administration, namely education, justice and political inclusion (or government competence); (2)

an underdeveloped political system, typically with an historical model of public governance, deeply characterized by theocratic influence (e.g. Somalia, Italy) or traditional legitimacy (e.g. Japan, Russia). Capitalism also fed contradictory and self-sabotaging stages in its implementation, reason why it is so antagonized, including the exploitation of labor, environmental impact, the lucrative trade of toxic products (tobacco, counterfeit fashion, chemicals etc.) and most importantly, market failure, which requires government intervention; such *vicious cycle* runs counter to the basic promise of the government, namely to reduce social evils and thus, it qualifies as a breach of the social contract.

In the crisis of epistemic and moral values, our society is characterized by the Golden Age of material values – what Plato called the "goods of the body" – namely wealth, health and strength in the lists of Hartmann and Frankena (materialism).

Freedom, the core value, also lay in economy: to be free, today, is to will & power, becoming rather than being, based purely on the extraction of resources and hedonistic capital, for public success.

Digital technology maximized the cosmetic tactics, eroding the *non-interference* (or freedom of choice) and in turn, promoting *short-termism.*

The first concept, I believe, is the result of a mechanistic world domination, where people are commodities themselves (by the ethics of beauty) and our wants are so manipulated (by the face value), so curated, that, at some point, it's no longer a meaningful choice; trends, wisdom of the crowd, the epistemic authority and ethical algorithms are just doing our reasoning for us, therefore, autonomy is essentially lost.

The second refers to an excessive focus on short-term results, at the expense of long-term goals, which consequently privileges the recent acquired taste for instant gratification, thus fostering the decline of quality in [personal and social relationships] life.

Prominent examples include the dedication and inclination to trust, honesty, intimacy, love, integrity, erudition and so on; all elements that take considerable time to develop but became quite rare.

Human traits - those values which are ascribed and said to define who we are, at the core, as human beings - consequently eroded. The value of a person is increasingly linked to his income level and public success; this trend distorts the classic meaning of "value", which should depend on the actions and power of "functions" exercised within a social network.

Bound for a new Renaissance, innovation and technology are also stimulating a subcultural preference for *spiritual, unique* human traits such as creativity, innovation, imagination, intercultural fluency, emotions, fears.

"The Agony of Eros" by Byung-Chul Han mapped the decline of love and desire in contemporary society, attributing it to the rise of individualism, capitalism and the "achievement society". Han posited that the relentless pursuit of self-optimization and the commodification of everything, including relationships, have led to a crisis where the "Other" is erased, and love is reduced to a form of self-consumption.

The Fourth Industrial Revolution marks the beginning of the Imagination Age, representing a comeback to a social and personal worth that bears meaning, rather than just result.

Still, deaestheticization looms large over the global society of post-cosmetics, not just a weak attempt to shift aesthetic focus on process over product but a nowhere-bound train, because true demateralization, although appealing in decentralized milieus - is form of obscurantism: worthless and pretend.

What's worse is that deaesthetization predates dehumanization, where individuals or groups are perceived as lacking unique qualities and are aesthetically (superficially) reduced to objects or means to an end. Virtue ethics is busy somewhere cogitating on whether AI could potentially develop superior moral virtues, and if so, whether humans should fear or embrace this new "ethical" being. The moral dilemma of artificial intelligence surpassing human morality is a fabricated dispute, because I hope humanity (and reality) will never completely be replaced by machine (and ideologies).

Apple just exposed the first real crack in the AI bubble in their latest paper, confirming there is no "thinking" happening in AI: it's all advanced pattern matching (like logic), which confirms that aesthetic norms are insufficient to deduce pure epistemic value. People are quietly asking if we are in the biggest bubble of history and all this aesthetic turn in epistemology was just a confidence game. Subject to all these considerations, value pluralism is the driving force of the axiological crisis and polarisation of contemporary society.

Due to the synchrony between the inevitable secularization of society and the persistent, human existential risk (whose engendered fragility still leads many to marry the possibility of spiritual transcendence, prominently religion or astrology), the present world amounts to an economic-social value system predicated on marketed individualism (or relativism), pitted against a doctrinal-political value system grounded in collectivism (or absolutism).

Forged epistemic values elaborated distorted ethical frameworks, a form of moral absolutism that aligned with populist rhetoric, assumptions that are fundamentally unsound which led to the marginalization of dissenting voices, shrinking of honest discourse on race, gender theory, public health risk management failures during migration and pandemic outbreaks, abortion, to name but a few. For instance, when the potential harms of technology such as privacy violations and algorithmic bias are overlooked in favour of perceived benefits - the aesthetic tactic of marketing. In 2004, Meskin forecast ethical values had become overly simplistic and reactive, failing to account for the nuances of social justice and equality.

Local values and traditions are overshadowed by dominant narratives that prioritize consumerism and individualism over community, and collective well-being.

The commodification of culture, cultural appropriation and the exploitation of marginalized communities have been central in the socio-anthropological debate against the Westernisation of the East, and how cultural homogenization proportionally relates to global wars, and conflicts.

Top-down effects of fabricated, epistemological absolutism are pervasive and removing known forgeries from epistemic value is insufficient to eradicate ethical absolutism, once constructed.

The outcome is rot and debasement of the epistemic system, while truth correspondence to reality is merely a cosmetic exercise.

Indirect doxastic voluntarism always makes us morally responsible for our beliefs, whose formation "politics" manifests a subliminal, greater freedom of thought than critical theorists credit human beings.

Our freedom to give in the "seductions of unreason" is the most stiff-necked adversary of thought, a creative skill people hone since childhood opportunistically and history is teeming with.

Critical theories, which often seek to challenge dominant power structures and highlight social injustices, fell into the trap of dogmatism. While they aim to promote social change, they inadvertently boosted forms of epistemological absolutism, by asserting that their critique is the only valid perspective.

As highlighted by Fritz, in 2016, postmodern views pilot dismissal of alternative viewpoints and a failure to engage in constructive dialogue (moral intransigence).

Richard Wolin's genealogy of post-truth spirit reminded postmodernism's infatuation with fascism has been extensive and widespread, that is, there's an illiberal intellectual lineage in light of the contemporary resurgence of political authoritarianism like cancel culture.

After all, it's the same "human infinite potentiality" postmodernists fought that pushed postmodern envelope, in the first place, offering laudable diagnoses of reality.

Crying against suppression stood often as just self-referential, diabolical covert narcissism too, rendering the whole individualistic enterprise ephemeral.

Excessive emphasis on subjective experiences and interpretations, while neglecting the role of objective evidence in reasoning, nurtures a fragmented understanding of knowledge, and morality; individuals feel justified in holding contradictory beliefs and mistaking truth, without the need for coherent justification.

Epistemic or moral paralysis ensues and nothing is true or false, no action can be deemed objectively wrong or right: all value judgments are seen as equally valid.

The large-scale moral effect of epistemological distortion, when it occurs, makes judicial judgments preposterous to be able to detect aesthetic falsifications of epistemic value, *a posteriori*, being subordinated within a political ethics of liability, purposely privileging oligarchy ($) and granting epistemic legitimacy (and authority) to the latter.

The immunity necessary under these conditions requires a highly refined critical perception, volitional control and a trained resistance to - an eye for - cosmetic tricks. Continued attention to value forgeries, once exposed, could help by increasing our search for authenticity, realism and epistemic prudence.

Disrupted aesthetic intuitions sow the seeds of our many existential commitments, in the same truth-bearing fashion, inflicting subtle epistemic damage and eventually prescribing how we should act, with a non-cognitivist flair, rather than describing objective epistemic and moral realities for the better.

| 7 |

The Art of Freedom

Realism, Debasement and Truth

My mega-deconstruction philosophical project began by addressing the types of epistemic attitudes toward "the beautiful" (metaphysically speaking, toward art) in an attempt to block out the normative element in them, with a wider gaze at value theory, and discuss how knowledge is a market economy.

Six pillars laid the groundwork for defining explanation (reasons why things happen), moral philosophy (reasons for action), and epistemology (reasons for belief).

It goes without saying that aesthetic experiences dictate our understanding and interpretation of truth, prominently nowadays, fomenting an epistemological clarification of the aesthetics as a mode of knowledge, in conditions of uncertainty.

Traditionally associated with taste, whatever pleases our mind is truth-apt, shaping our epistemic framework, even if facts contradict, because we opportunistically need it to serve our immediate purpose and strategies.

Value has long been intertwined with the theoretical pursuit of truth and moral ideals, vis a vis the satisfaction of practical reasons and personal interests, setting the stage for inevitable reflection on normative conflict.

Aesthetic sources fundamentally warrant ethical norms: inasmuch as predispositions, epistemic attitudes are a type of ethical conditions, that is, somebody's epistemology can be defined in terms of principles, habits or method too, just like lately, aesthetic concepts (ideals of beauty) have come to stand as ethical norms.

Our aesthetic attitudes (taste) allow for the formation of epistemic norms (standards) related to things like belief, knowledge, and reasoning, overall composing our code of conduct (ethics), from good/bad belief (epistemological ethics) to good/bad action (normative ethics).

Aesthetic and epistemic values conflict, when an aesthetic appeal overrides truth or moral considerations, building a normative fork.

Conflict between aesthetic, epistemic and moral values are acute within contemporary society, automating pervasive distortions - termed "value forgeries" - that undermine truth, authenticity, and normative standards. Debasement or devaluation is commonplace.

System theory reflection encapsulated the core of our epistemic crisis in the digital age, how aesthetic judgments drive misunderstanding of epistemic values, simulated images and narratives distort standards of truth (and consequently, morality), in a hyper social world, where everything people do becomes custom - even falsus transforms into ethos.

Let's recapitulate the lie of the land:

Value Generation through Aesthetic Engagement

Aesthetic engagement triggers epistemic value attribution blending different forms of reasoning, from aesthetic, logical, epistemic to ethical, up and including illogical. There is power in aesthetics to pilot understanding of epistemic values, upgrading or downgrading knowledge, justification, reason, correctness, moral objectivity, therefore norm generation.

Practical and theoretical reasoning meet under a common epistemic norm, aesthetic experiences contribute to the normative framework by serving as a means of generating knowledge as much as nescience.

The Role of Uncertainty in Aesthetic Judgment

In conditions of uncertainty, aesthetics serves as the heuristic for navigating the unknown. Aesthetic experiences guide individuals in making sense of ambiguous situations, helping them to construct meaning with emotional, and imaginative weight. Aesthetic judgments provide insights into epistemic value, particularly in contexts where empirical evidence is incomplete.

Aesthetic Experience as Manipulation of Value

Knowledge (will) alters in its expression (art): our understanding of existence is not fixed but can be shaped through perception, culture, and language (epistemic facelifts), whose resulting manipulation brings about distorted views of what is real (augmented reality).

The truth-value of a belief always constitutes its ultimate worth-value, rejecting the correspondence theory of truth in favour of perspectivism. Cosmetic epistemology refers to presenting epistemic values (knowledge, justification, truth) in a way that is reasonably palatable or attractive, while obscuring deeper incorrectness. Superficial understandings mask underlying complexities, because what we choose to consider true is swept by personal, practical, random or social agendas.

The art of rhetoric can be seen as a tool for, logically speaking, "corrupting existence" by persuading others to accept a manipulated version of p, often for ideological or personal gain.

Normative Implications of Cosmetic Reasons

When faced with practical interests, aesthetic experiences turn individuals away from informed and reflective judgments, governing the normative nature of all existential commitments such as epistemic, ethical, social or political. Aesthetics is the fountainhead of epistemic value and reason has many talents: embodied, social, political, opportunistic. The inevitable normativity of aesthetic reasons always trump our epistemic and moral judgments. Knowledge is saturated with beauty: positive or negative aesthetic normativity sets the ball of epistemic normativity rolling and, in time, its ethical qualities - a norm is a pattern even if negative, irrational, fake.

There's a deliberative socio-political constraint on normativity, the power in the principles (truth value) is deeply tied to the way in which they are represented (aesthetic normativity).

Instrumentalism and Aesthetic Normativity

Steglich-Petersen's work on epistemic instrumentalism supports the view that aesthetic reasons can be understood as instrumental in "framing" knowledge and belief formation (consequently morality and actions), rather than being a mere accessory to truth, principally when navigating uncertainty or at the mercy of practical interests.

Value corruption spreads a moral failing — epistemic distortions eventually deliver harmful outcomes during the transmission, affecting individuals and societies, by manifolding. Corrupting the existential import of x in a model urges reflection on ethical responsibilities in how we present epistemic values. Facts can be separated from values but aesthetics (and cosmetics) is instrumental in affirming alethic monism. Before AI, we already deliberated with fact-insensitivity.

Consistency and Coherence in Epistemic Reasoning and Ethical Normativity

Aesthetics (and cosmetic tactics) play an explanatory role in epistemic reasoning, especially when individuals are faced with conflicting evidence, or bias. The failings of analytic philosophy and any attempt to "naturalizing" philosophy are notable, because "feelings are not facts", yet "facts do not change our mind", thus objectivity hardly coheres with our egonomics. Especially in view of epistemic risks, contractualism is the most fitting approach, in moral theory.

Existential Enquiry

Value alteration creates disconnection or existential alienation, as individuals grapple with conflicting perceptions of p's existence. At large, what it means to live authentically in a world where existence can be corrupted stands for how to discern genuine experiences from manipulated ones. It's a human struggle to find meaning in a world that can be chaotically meaningless and deceptive, challenging individuals to create their own understanding of existence, amidst *debasement*.

The value dilemma resonates with postmodern ideas about the fluidity of truth and the skepticism toward grand narratives, while calibrating the fragmented nature of knowledge, and relative morality. Scientific enquiry cannot be value-neutral and existentialist themes of absurdity, the search for meaning, in the face of an often irrational and deceptive world shall be recognized.

Epistemic Pluralism: The Missing Link and the Ambitions of Epistemology

Epistemological pluralism is to be distinguished from ontological pluralism, the study of different modes of being, for example, the contrast in the mode of existence exhibited by "numbers", with that of "people" or "cars".

In the philosophy of science, epistemological pluralism arose in opposition to reductionism to express the contrary view that, at least some natural phenomena cannot be fully explained by a single theory or be fully investigated, using a single approach.

In economics, controversy persists between using a single epistemological approach or a variety.

Reading between the lines, I juxtaposed competing dimensions of realism in philosophy, from classical and scientific realism to contemporary, fine-grained orientations like critical, structural realism and meta-realism. The excursus evinced domineering forms of realism such as naïve, scientific, and phenomenological, however, there remain other germane approaches that could serve as valuable benchmarks for accounting the dauntingly ineffable interaction between perception, representation, and truth.

As previously canvassed, it's not been easy to define how we acquire, generate and transmit knowledge for normative purposes: individualist perspectivism (and left-wing, post-modernism), collectivist perspectivism (power-oriented view, and focus on consciousness), pragmatism (and identity through time) verificationism (science and explanatory gap) arguably stepped forward to report a comprehensive rationale.

I could not appraise all the ontological variants of idealism, phenomenalism, instrumentalism and constructivism, rather I chose to put meta-realism, conceptual and structural realism, critical and dialectical critical realism, speculative realism (and off-springs) through their paces, because my line of argument grows right out these.

A present-day movement, meta-realism sees reality as a layered or hierarchical infrastructure, where metaphysical realities or multiple structures underpin our immediate experience.

Since each layer or construction of reality may itself be subject to further interpretation, such overarching account of reality is a breeding ground of vagueness and ambiguity: an infinite regress with no clear criteria for what constitutes "truth" or "knowledge", therefore no objectivity.

In aesthetics, metarealism denies that our perceptions or representations may truly access the world, thus authentically depict or represent reality.

Its skeptical contour relativizes the meaning and value of art (free will): from aesthetic judgements to epistemic normativity.

Whilst not explicitly labeled a meta-realist, Kant's critical philosophy firstly introduced the layered view of reality, with the distinction between *noumenal* (things-in-themselves) and *phenomenal* (appearances), although the former is basically inaccessible.

His thesis on the limits of human knowledge and the constructed nature of experience is the most important harbinger of metarealism.

On the Kantian wave, empiricism and ordinary language philosophies, like G. E. Moore and Bertrand Russell's, became the workhorses of realism, using the primacy of ordinary language and empirical verification to resist the Hegelian idea of layered, hierarchical realities beyond observable phenomena.

Existentialism, phenomenalism, instrumentalism spearheaded the revolt against realism, contra the certainty that physical objects exist independently of our minds, and that our perceptions of them are generally accurate representations of how they are in themselves. An ontologically privileged, "meta" level of reality kicked in, under the aegis of psychology, constructivism, hyperrealism and critical theories.

In recent years, philosophical postures attempted to synthesize ideas from both the analytic tradition (logical clarity, language, science) and the continental tradition (phenomenology, existentialism, hermeneutics, and critique of scientific reductionism).

Taking up the gauntlet, conceptual realism honed the flaws of classical realism to bring objective back into subjective Discourse: maintaining the layered, often metaphorical view of reality, dear to antirealist currents, its developer Wilfrid Sellars argued that our perceptions are mediated by conceptual frameworks, therefore proving the real, universal existence of objects, concepts, and particulars within a synthetic, metaphysical theory.

A leading figure in critical realism, Bhaskar's philosophy opposed layered reality with structures that exist independently but are often inaccessible directly, stitching together both crutch points.

On tenterhooks, the vast landscape of interdisciplinary realism continues to produce a welter of alternative metaphysics.

Followed by Isabelle Stengers, William Desmond, Alfred North Whitehead's process philosophy astound with a post-analytic concept of reality that is dynamic and interconnected, sprouting the layered and relational nature of existence.

The tenets of process ontology are becoming, change and interconnectedness: reality is fundamentally dynamic, processual, and relational rather than static or substance-based.

From an analytic perspective, process philosophy aligns with scientific understandings of the world as dynamic, interconnected systems, incorporating formal models and logical analysis.

From a continental perspective, the vision makes sense too because it does not drop the transcendental project, resonating with phenomenological and existential themes of becoming, temporality, and the primacy of experience, and relations.

Promising candidates for a comprehensive, integrative theory of reality that suits both traditions also include contemporary speculative realism, object-oriented ontology (OOO), relational or network ontologies - bloomed more or less in that order.

Key figures like Quentin Meillassoux, Graham Harman, Levi Bryant judge reality as fundamentally constituted by relations, processes or networks, rather than static substances: the external world consists of objects that exist independently of human perception, with a focus on their vitality, beyond human understanding.

Inspired by David Chalmers's work on consciousness as a fundamental feature of reality (panta rei), and Bruno Latour's actor-network theory, these holistic philosophical trends are compatible with both analytic, scientific methodologies (e.g. systems theory, network analysis) and continental, pluralistic outlooks.

Anthropocentric and linguistic constraints of traditional philosophy are surpassed: formal rigor meets experiential and hermeneutic depth, moving beyond traditional metarealist approaches.

Be that as it may, critics argue that process philosophy is overly abstract, with an inherent difficulty in empirical verification and concrete application of hypotheses.

William P. Alston confuted Whitehead's metaphysical claims as insufficiently rigorous.

Many contend speculative realism too is abstract or conjectural, lacking clear criteria for evaluating claims about reality, independent of human access.

Scientists and philosophers of sciences bashed its exponents as overly concerned with metaphysical speculation.

Timothy Williamson detected a lack of empirical grounding and E.J. Lowe posited that speculative realists neglect the importance of human cognition, and scientific methodology.

Academic cavillers didn't even spare object-oriented ontology (OOO), lambasting it as inaccessible or seemingly obscure.

As a matter of fact, treating all entities as equally real and autonomous risks collapsing into a form of "everything is an object" (pan-objectivism), which may diminish distinctions between different kinds of entities.

Bruno Latour panned the OOO for ignoring the relational and networked aspects of objects, that is, for neglecting the role of human and social factors. Whilst not directly attacking it, in the same vein, Alain Badiou found fault with philosophies that detach objects from their evental, and relational contexts, encouraging semi-realism.

Many analytic philosophers and scientists concluded that OOO's metaphysics is speculative too, lacking empirical support or clear scientific applicability like the other contemporary, integrative theories of reality.

Semi-realism, a philosophical stance that aims to be a more modest form of scientific realism, faces challenges in defining the boundaries of what is considered "real" and what is not.

The receivers struggle with solving regular issues like distinguishing between observable and unobservable entities, explaining how theoretical claims can be both empirically successful and false, and justifying the selective retention of certain theoretical components while discarding others.

I subscribe to all those reservations and have a definitive halfway house to counteroffer but time (and space) of this foundation prequel is over, so I defer its elaboration to my breakthrough philosophical work, coming next.

Sources

- [1,2] Introduction from Achille Virzi, *"The World in Focus: Stories of Hallucinations and Philosophical Myopia"*, 2010
- en.wikipedia.org
- www.thenation.com
- philosophybreak.com
- ebin.pub
- philevents.org
- philpapers.org
- wikimili.com
- johnquiggin.com
- stanrock.net
- amedleyofpotpourri.blogspot.com
- Edward Waters College on 2025-09-09
- graphsearch.ep .ch
- www.bbc.co.uk
- www.perfectcircuit.com
- eek.ipfs.io
- philarchive.org
- www.columbia.edu
- www.britannica.com
- The University of Memphis on 2025-03-04
- Amity University on 2014-03-28
- dialogic.blogspot.com
- Suleyman Demirel University, Kazakhstan on 2020-05-05
- alwaysbeast.net
- www.livelaptopspec.com
- Vermont State Colleges on 2019-10-21
- readonlinefree.net
- www.absoluteastronomy.com
- www.researchwithrutgers.com
- www.amazon.com
- University of Nottingham on 2025-03-18
- igorgoldkind.com

- Intercollege on 2023-02-25
- www.coursehero.com
- scienceoxygen.com
- KCA University on 2025-04-23
- Republic Polytechnic on 2014-12-10 <1%
- University of Westminster on 2020-12-06 40
- bmcr.brynmawr.edu
- Doncaster College, South Yorkshire on 2012-11-24
- hbr.org
- bogreolen.dk
- Reinhardt University on 2022-06-09
- South Island School on 2023-07-14
- www.newyorker.com
- University of Birmingham on 2021-01-30
- orca.cardi .ac.uk
- www.adb.org 52
- www.ielts-mentor.com
- download.bibis.ir
- users.tpg.com.au
- www.project-syndicate.org
- CSU, San Jose State University on 2025-03-12
- Singapore Institute of Technology on 2019-04-01
- Central Queensland University on 2014-04-15
- University of Hong Kong on 2024-02-27
- mediationsjournal.org
- www.adamwalanus.pl
- Aspen University on 2024-09-10
- Forsyth County Academy on 2023-11-13
- Charles City High School on 2010-01-14
- National College of Ireland on 2014-11-21
- Republic Polytechnic on 2014-06-13
- University of Houston System on 2018-09-25
- www.quotescosmos.com
- uwe-repository.worktribe.com
- vdoc.pub
- Stan Patton, www.stanrock.net
- www.investigo.biblioteca.uvigo.es

References and Bibliography

- Georg Wilhelm Friedrich Hegel, *The Phenomenology of Spirit,* 1807
- Martin Heidegger, *Being and Time*, 1927
- Jean-Paul Sartre, *Being and Nothingness*, 1943
- George Orwell, *Animal Farm*, 1945
- Max Horkheimer and Theodor W. Adorno, *Dialectic of Enlightenment*, 1947
- Solomon Asch, *Studies of Independence and Conformity: I. A Minority of One Against a Unanimous Majority*, 1956
- Roland Barthes, *Mythologies*, 1957
- Donald Davidson, *Radical Interpretation*, 1973
- Michael Stocker, *The Schizophrenia of Modern Ethical Theories*, 1976
- Nelson Goodman, *Ways of Worldmaking*, 1978
- Tyler Burge, *Individualism and the Mental*, 1979
- Saul Kripke, *Naming and Necessity*, 1980
- Daniel Kahneman, Paul Slovic, Amos Tversky, *Judgment Under Uncertainty: Heuristics and Biases*, 1982
- Harry Frankfurt, *On Bullshit*, 1986
- Roy Bhaskar, *Reclaiming Reality*, 1989
- Ned Block & Hilary Putnam, *Representation and Philosophy of Mind*, 1991
- David Paxman, *Aesthetics as Epistemology, or Knowledge without Certainty*, 1993
- Al-Issa, Ihsan, *The Illusion of Reality or the Reality of Illusion: Hallucinations and Culture*, 1995
- David Johnson, *Conventionalism about Logical Truth*, Philosophical Topics, 1995
- Thomas Donaldson, *Values in Tension: Ethics Away from Home*, 1996
- Stanislas Dehaene, The Number Sense, 1996
- George Lakoff and Rafael E. Núñez, Where Mathematics Comes From, 2000
- David Graeber, *Toward an Anthropological Theory of Value*, 2001
- F. Geyer, in *International Encyclopedia of the Social & Behavioral Sciences*, 2001
- Steven Pinker, *The Blank Slate: The Modern Denial of Human Nature*, 2002
- Umberto Eco, *On Ugliness,* 2002

- Gabriele Palombo, *Il mal di vivere dell'uomo moderno. Saggi di antropologia personalistica*, 2005
- Keith Devlin, *The Math Instinct*, 2005
- Jason Stanley, *Knowledge and Practical Interests*, 2005
- Michael A. Bishop and J. D. Trout, *Epistemology and the Psychology of Human Judgment*, 2005
- WH Wong, *The skeptical paradox and the indispensability of knowledge-beliefs*, 2005
- Cristiano Castelfranchi, *Six critical remarks on science and the construction of the knowledge society. Journal of Science Communication*, 2007
- Elliott Sober, *Evidence and Evolution: The Logic Behind the Science*, 2008
- Dan Gardner, *Risk: The Science and Politics of Fear*, 2008
- Achille Varzi, *The World in Focus. Stories of Philosophical Hallucinations and Myopias*, 2010
- David Chalmers, *Constructing the World*, 2012
- Eliot Aronson, Timothy Wilson, Robin Akert, *Conformity: Influencing Behavior*, 2013
- Stephen Franzoi, *Social Influence*, 2013
- Alissa Quart, Adventures in Neurohumanities, The Nation, 8 May 2013
- Seán Moran, *Knowledge from Testimony: Benefits and Dangers*, 2013
- Penelope Rush, *Introduction. The Metaphysics of Logic*, 2014
- Bernd R. Hornung, in *International Encyclopedia of the Social & Behavioral Sciences*, 2015
- *The Oxford Handbook of Hypo-egoic phenomena*, 2016
- Jennifer M. Harris and Robert D. Blackwill, *War by Other Means: Geoeconomics and Statecraft*, 2016
- Saiyin Sun, *Beyond the Iron House - Lu Xun and the Modern Chinese Literary Field*, Routledge, 2016
- Susanna S. Epp, *Proof Issues with Existential Quantification*, 2016
- Jack M Gorman and Sara E. Gorman, *Denying to the Grave: Why We Ignore the Facts That Will Save Us*, 2016
- Richard Prumm, *The Evolution of Beauty: How Darwin's Forgotten Theory of Mate Choice Shapes the Animal World – And Us*, 2017
- Joe L. Kincheloe, *Knowledge and Critical Pedagogy: An Introduction.*, 2017
- Jack Donnelly, *Cultural Relativism and Universal Human Rights*, 2017
- Hugo Mercier and Dan Sperber, *The Enigma of Reason*, 2017
- Broad Ellen, *Made by Humans: The Ai Condition*, 2018
- John Quiggin, *Will a robot take your job?*, September 2018
- Erik and others Born, *The Creativity Complex*, 2018

- Ralph Wedgwood, *Epistemic Teleology: Synchronic and Diachronic*, 2018
- Philip Fernbach and Steven Sloman, *The Knowledge Illusion: Why We Never Think Alone,* Riverhead, 2018
- Heather Widdows, *Perfect Me. Beauty as an Ethical Ideal, 2019*
- David Michael Levin, *The Listening Self. Personal Growth, Social Change and the Closure of Metaphysics*, 1989 - 2019
- Amy Latessa, *Fascism, Imperialism, and the Reclamation of Italian Masculinity from Ethiopia, 1935–1941,* University of Cincinnati, 2019
- David Michael Levin, The Listening Self. Personal Growth, Social Change and the Closure of Metaphysics, 1989-2019
- Martin Kush, *"Psychologism"* in The Stanford Encyclopedia of Philosophy, 2020
- Michael Rescorla, *"Convention"* in The Stanford Encyclopedia of Philosophy, 2021
- Michael Peters, *Nāgārjuna – 'Wittgenstein, Nāgārjuna and relational quantum mechanics*, Educational Philosophy and Theory, Volume 54, Issue 12, Taylor & Francis, 2022
- Gilles Kassel, *A plea for epistemic ontologies*, 2023
- Christopher K. McDonnell, *The Visual Language of Cartoon Eyes Aesthetics & Associations of Eye Design in Animated Characters*, Drexel University , 2025

Letter to Gettier

ORIGINAL MESSAGES

Sent: Friday, February 14, 2020 9:15 PM
To: UMass Amherst Alumni Association **<alumni@admin.umass.edu>**
Subject: Form submission from: Contact UMass Amherst

I would like to get in touch with Mr. Professor Emeritus Edmund Gettier to deliver a post-graduation message and thank him for his contributions to philosophy, which greatly inspired my study. Tried to use his faculty email but it does not exist. Could you please assist?

Thank you
Vincent

On Wed, 19 Feb 2020 at 19:33,

On Wed, 19 Feb 2020 at 19:33, UMass Amherst Alumni Association <alumni@ad-min.umass.edu> wrote:

Vincent,

Thanks for your email

Due to privacy laws, we are unable to provide the contact information for Prof. Gettier to you.

If you would like to send an email to me, I could print it out and mail it to him or send a letter in the mail to me and I could send it to him. He does not have an active email address on file.

Please, let me know how I can assist you further.

Go UMass!!
Deb Warnick
UMass Amherst Alumni Relations
Memorial Hall, 134 Hicks Way
Amherst, MA 01003-9270

To
Prof. Emeritus Edmund Gettier
University of Massachusetts

L *ondon, 18th November 2019*

Dear Prof. Gettier,

my name is Vincent, a London-based philosophy sophomore.

I decided to personally write, as I am about to graduate and I wish to acknowledge you as one of my models in modern academia (along Grayling, Chomsky, Blackburn, historian James Turner, to name but a few).

Your landmark essay had a profound impact on my dialectical maturity; your maverick approach to research writing affected my wild clarity, driving away genetical logorrheic temptations.

Although I ended up progressing so far into higher education, I suffer the hostility of academic politics, for its staunch submission to formalism and boredom. This is partly why, I am working in a complete, different sector and I prefer to be a philosopher "super partes", away from titles and papers.

Too many intellectuals are best known for long, dense articles, sometimes just made of recycled, third-party concepts and I sadly gathered they all seem to be following the same modus operandi: creative ambition was professionally drained out of such a wonderful "path of life" that is the one of a thinker, who shall be inherently free from structures and constraints.

Thus, when the number of essays became the requirement and the index score the only measure of my academic value, your bold, unorthodox synthesis (as opposed to the typical professorial redundancy, and loads of paid features few read), inflamed my fire to swim upstream.

We can thank humanists, both past and present, for a number of our deeply held beliefs. I can say today your implicit lesson in brevity motivates how sharp my scholarship aspires to be, how offbeat I bravely walk the field and how I understand, and interact with the broader classism of universities, out there.

A writer or a philosopher must set new trends like delivering quality of work, instead of mass producing academese for salary upgrade. You stuck up for it and I thank you for reminding me that I am on the right track, that my non-conformism too may be a strength in academic circles and to push my awkward way, whenever I feel wrong, lonely or less than "honor students".

Aware of the fact that you probably do not have time to peruse on my intrusion - somewhat abstruse - I wanted to sincerely wish you well and continued strength in navigating health issues.

N.B. Rather than tertiary or quaternary, what if there is no structure to knowledge, at all?

Kind Regards,
Vincent Bozzino

www.ingramcontent.com/pod-product-compliance
Lightning Source LLC
Chambersburg PA
CBHW071932090426
42811CB00042B/2421/J